Stepping Stones
along the path of life

52 Week Devotional

Andrew P. Surace

Stepping Stones

along the path of life

52 WEEK DEVOTIONAL

ANDREW P. SURACE

MorningStar Publications
A DIVISION OF MORNINGSTAR FELLOWSHIP CHURCH
P.O. Box 440
Wilkesboro, NC 28697

Stepping Stones Along the Path of Life
Andrew P. Surace
Copyright © 2005

International Standard Book Number—1-929371-52-7

All Scriptures are New International Version unless otherwise indicated.

Photography/Cover Design/Inside Layout: Sharon Whitby

DEDICATION

To the Father, Son, and Holy Ghost, Who never
give up on leading me to the way I should go.

❖

To Rick Joyner, for believing in my work
and encouraging me to continue.

❖

To my father, who taught me about keeping my focus
and the importance of taking risks when necessary.

❖

To my wife, Kathleen, whose love and support
encourage me daily—especially her ability to
give me space, while never letting me feel alone.

❖

To my precious children: Gabriella, Bethanie, Andrew,
Ryan, Jenna, and Melissa, you are all beautiful works
of God and I love you all more than you will ever know.
The best is yet to come.

❖

To my executive assistant, Traci, for all the help
and encouragement you have given Kathleen and I
along the way, and, of course, your proofreading.

❖

To Covenant Life Church, for being a
strong body of faithful believers who are
living for something worth dying for.

❖

To all those who have provided bits and pieces
of inspiration in my life and have never known it.

TABLE OF CONTENTS

PREFACE

Writing this book has been a little like going on a cross-country trip—not quite knowing what will be seen or encountered along the way. After writing the first book, *Power Points from the Word*, you would think the process would be fairly unremarkable. The good news is that it was not. Each devotion has brought new and rich insights into my life, and it is my prayer it will do the same for you.

Once again, God has been gracious in helping me to turn some of the pain and obstacles in my life into gain, and hopefully, it will help others dealing with similar situations. Like *Power Points from the Word*, this book was written mostly in the wee hours of the morning (between 3 a.m. and 6 a.m.) during a time when the phone does not ring and the kids are not calling.

My two sons, both of whom are fishermen, are one of the reasons I am up early in the morning. The click of the door between 3 a.m. and 4 a.m. reminds me it is time to pray for their safety. That is the beginning of many thoughts and ideas that need to be put on paper or, in this case, typed into a laptop. It is interesting how God uses every area of our lives for His purpose if we allow Him to do this.

While I am not sure how many more books of this type I will be able to write, it is my desire as you read this one, for you to know that God's principles are the same yesterday, today, and forever. What He did for Moses and Paul, He will do for you and me. God's wisdom works in all situations, for all people, and at all times. Again, all we must do is ask God for His wisdom. Remember, we have not because we ask not (see James 4:2).

Although this book was written as a 52-week devotional, it has been my experience that most people read it daily. No matter what your style, get the most out of each chapter. God has great things in store for your life and having knowledge of His Word is necessary to obtain them. It is my prayer that this book will help teach you how to deal with everyday situations so that they will not become obstacles, but rather stepping stones to greater victories in your life.

Andrew P. Surace

WEEK 1

THE SWORD OF THE LORD AND GIDEON

**When I blow with a trumpet, I and all
that are with me, then blow ye the trumpets
also on every side of all the camp, and say,
The sword of the LORD, and of Gideon.**

Judges 7:18 (KJV)

Here we see the combination that God used throughout the Bible and even today—a holy God working through an imperfect and fragile human. Gideon is like many of us in that he did not think too much of himself. Psychologists would say he did not have a good self-image. By the way, the opposite of that could be equally as dangerous. Most of the time when we have a bad image of ourselves it is because we leave God out of the picture. Admittedly, if we look at ourselves without God, there is not really much good to see. However, when we join ourselves to God there is not much we cannot do.

God found Gideon threshing wheat in a wine press trying to hide it from the Midianites. An angel greeted him by saying **"the Lord is with thee, thou mighty man of valor" (Judges 6:12 KJV)**. Needless to say, Gideon did not know to whom he was talking. It reminds me of a Three Stooges episode when a man walked into the room and addressed the Stooges as

"Gentlemen." They looked around with incredulous looks on their faces, saying, "Where? Where?" Gideon did not think he was a man of valor any more than the Three Stooges thought they were gentlemen. The key is that God called him a man of valor because God saw his potential, not his present situation. The name Gideon means "warrior" and that is the way God saw him. He did not see a man hiding and trying to gather a few crumbs to feed his family, but a mighty warrior who would help deliver God's people from their bondage.

> *God does not look at where we are but where He's called us to be.*

God does not look at where we are but where He's called us to be. He did this with Moses, David, and many others in the Bible who had looked to themselves for answers but kept coming up empty. God often chooses the least likely person to get the job done, so when the job gets done, He gets all the glory. Maybe you are facing a situation that you know you just do not have the ability to handle. My friend, this is God's way of drawing you to Himself. God very rarely calls us to do that which we are capable, but rather He calls us to do that which is impossible for us by ourselves. Through this He brings us into a partnership with Him.

Although God could save the world and lead the church without us, He chooses to do it through us. In return He asks that we give Him all the honor and glory. Would you allow God to work His perfect will through you? This way, He can touch people around you and they will realize **"how lovely on the mountains are the feet of him who brings good news (Isaiah 52:7 NAS),"** and also He who sent them.

WEEK 2

WHEN HE CAME TO HIS SENSES

**"When he came to his senses, he said,
'How many of my father's hired men have food
to spare, and here I am starving to death!'"
Luke 15:17**

The story of the prodigal son should serve as a reminder to us of the damage and pain we can inflict on ourselves and others when we run off without the leading of the Holy Spirit. The deception we can fall into when we entertain thoughts about the things of this world, while pushing aside the wisdom and guidance of the Holy Spirit, is almost mind-altering.

Have you ever looked back on a particular time in your life at some of the crazy things you have been involved in and said to yourself "what in the world was I thinking?" I can honestly say that when I look back at some of the things I did and some of the decisions I made in my younger years, I honestly think aliens came and kidnapped my brain. Then, just to really make me look like a fool, they gave it back. I think you know what I am saying. Living life outside the leading of the Holy Spirit can be treacherous and painful. So how do we keep from losing our senses and perhaps many other precious things in our lives? God has given us many safeguards to keep that which has been given to us. However, like all things in our walk with God, it will take faith and obedience.

The first thing God has given us to keep our lives in check is His Word. Be sure to check your plans with the Word of God. Satan will often wave counterfeits in front of our eyes hoping we will focus on them and not the Word of God. The son in this story obviously was not led by the Word of God, but rather his feelings. Feelings do have a function in our lives, but guidance is not one of them. Remember, as we walk by faith and obedience, good feelings are a by-product of that faith.

Feelings do have a function in our lives but guidance is not one of them.

God also promises that the Holy Spirit will be our guide. Learn to cultivate sensitivity to the Holy Spirit. That still, small voice can keep you from being a large, moving target for the enemy. Although God will always forgive us of our sins and mistakes if we come humbly to Him and confess them, we will lose much valuable ground if we walk in our own strength. God forgives sins, but we must live with the consequences.

The last thing we can do to protect ourselves from the deception of the enemy is to honor those God has put in authority over us. In each of our lives, God puts people with wisdom to help guide us through the hardships of life. It can be parents, pastors, friends, or relatives. The Bible teaches us "**...in the multitude of counselors there is safety**" (**Proverbs 11:14** NKJV). If you are not sure of an upcoming decision, check with those God has put over you who speak into your life. Those in authority over us are there to help protect and guide us through the minefields of life.

In closing, I find it beautiful that even after the enemy had stolen everything from this young man, the one thing he could not take was his memory. When he came to his senses and *remembered* the peace and prosperity of his father's house, he returned home. Maybe you have strayed far from the love of your family or your heavenly Father. Just take time now to remember how much you are loved; it is not too late to turn things around. We serve an awesome God, Who is able to turn even the worst situations around for our good if we choose to live for Him. It may not be easy, but there is only one path that leads to life. I pray today that you will get back on this path and let God begin to restore the things that the enemy has stolen from your life.

WEEK 3

THE THREAT
OF UNITY

**And the LORD came down to see the city and
the tower, which the children of men builded.**

**And the LORD said, Behold, the people is one,
and they have all one language; and this they
begin to do: and now nothing will be restrained
from them, which they have imagined to do.**

Genesis 11:5-6 (KJV)

Nothing scares Satan more than the thought of unity in
the kingdom. Good theology, beautiful buildings, even
great music can never bring about the power that unity can
bring. Remember, one can chase a thousand, and two can
put ten thousand to flight (see Deuteronomy 32:30). Satan
fights viciously against unity because he knows it is the
atomic bomb of the kingdom.

Throughout the book of Acts we can see the unity principle at work. God's power came only after His people stood
in unity. Christ's prayer in John 17 was that His believers
would be one, even as He and the Father were one. In Paul's
letters to the church at Corinth, he pleaded with them to be
in unity and put an end to the constant strife and division.
Whether the project is good or bad it cannot be accomplished
without unity.

In the introductory passage, we see the tremendous potential of unity. The first thing we see is that the whole earth spoke one language. Because of this, there was tremendous power in their speech. There was no wasted time trying to figure out what the other person wanted. A command was given and a command was obeyed. In fact, these people were in so much unity that they caught the attention of God. As a little side note, unity always catches God's attention.

Unity is the example God gave us and it's the only way to bring power back into the church.

We read further in verse six that God said because they were in such great unity, they would be able to accomplish whatever they imagined. As I stated earlier, even if the desire is evil, unity will help bring it to pass. This is actually what got God involved. It was not so much the evil of the project, but the unity of the people.

Think about what the church could accomplish if they were in unity. Imagine the battles that could be won if the church was one. This is why Satan fights so hard against unity. If the church had unity, it could accomplish whatever it desired. Satan knows this because he saw what happened with the Tower of Babel. The only way God stopped them from accomplishing their desire was to confuse their language. One guy asks for a brick, he gets a tomato. Another asks for a hammer, he gets a kiss. You get the picture.

Unfortunately, this is a picture of the modern day church. Baptists have their language. Fundamentalists have their language. Charismatics have their language. A new believer walks into the church and asks for a Bible and he's told, "Only read King James, it's what Jesus would have used."

So begins the indoctrination of religion—a system of beliefs and doctrines instead of a family built on love, grace, and unity. Now the church, instead of being a giant force to be reckoned with, becomes a weak, watered down organization looking for people to support its own belief system. Instead of being a lifesaving station, it has become a station on life support. Unity is the example God gave us and it is the only way to bring power back into the church. What are you doing to make it happen?

WEEK 4

STRANGERS IN THE NIGHT

That they may keep thee from the
strange woman, from the stranger
which flattereth with her words.

For at the window of my house
I looked through my casement,

and beheld among the simple ones,
I discerned among the youths,
a young man void of understanding,

passing through the street near her corner;
and he went the way to her house,

in the twilight, in the evening,
in the black and dark night."

Proverbs 7:5-9 (KJV)

LUST. It has started wars, brought down kingdoms, destroyed families, made orphans of children, and brought more pain into the world than any of us would like to think about. Most of the people reading this have either been or known someone who has been a victim of this dangerous sin. As a sin, it ranks up there with murder, idolatry, and some of life's other major destroyers.

First, I must make it clear that you can lust after many things including cars, homes, power, money, and so on.

However, in this devotion, I am only talking about lust that leads to sexual immorality. It may start with an innocent glance or a simple conversation, but if it is allowed to fester it could lead to the destruction of all that we know as good. Yet, despite the damage that lust causes and the many biblical warnings to beware of it, it still goes relatively unnoticed and unchecked in the lives of many Christians.

Proverbs makes an interesting point on the subject of sexual sin (see Proverbs 5:22-23). God allows someone to fall into sexual immorality when his or her continuous sin and rebellion reaches a certain level. It is almost as if you do not choose this lifestyle, it chooses you. Ecclesiastes 7:26 goes on to say that if a man's ways please God, he will not fall into this horrible pit. Please note that God does not make the decision as to who falls into the pit, but we do by either obeying or disobeying God in our lifestyles. We are not victims of circumstance, but victims of our choices.

> *We are not victims of circumstance but victims of our choices.*

The Bible does not just warn us about this type of sin, but also gives us some good advice on how to deal with it. First, like all sins, lust begins in the mind. This is why we must renew our minds daily by the washing of the Word of God. God's Word has a cleansing effect on all we think or say. When God's Word becomes ingrained in our hearts, it helps flush out the seeds the enemy daily tries to plant. We also see that the Word teaches us to avoid, whenever possible, those who lead sensual, rebellious lifestyles. Proverbs 5:8 states, **"remove thy way far from her, and come not nigh the door of her house (KJV)."** Ungodly influences will almost always corrupt good behavior.

Finally, as a last resort, the Bible says to run if you still find yourself in a place of great sexual temptation. I like to call this the Joseph principle. When Potiphar's wife attempted to seduce Joseph, he did not try to figure out what she was doing or why she was doing it, he just ran. The Bible tells us to flee fornication and youthful lusts (see II Timothy 2:22). There are certain sins that God does not want you to stick around and battle. I can only assume that the reason He tells us to run from these situations is because sexual sins appeal to every part of our sinful, human nature. Therefore, the odds of victory are not good without divine intervention. I do also want to mention that although God's grace is always sufficient, wisdom dictates flight in some circumstances. So the next time you meet a stranger in the night and sparks are beginning to fly, just remember that small sparks can start a great fire, and there are times when flight is better than fight.

WEEK 5

NEBUCHADNEZZAR MY SERVANT

**Then say to them, "This is what the
Lord Almighty, the God of Israel, says:
I will send for my servant Nebuchadnezzar
king of Babylon, and I will set his throne
over these stones I have buried here; he will
spread his royal canopy above them."**
Jeremiah 43:10

"**M**y servant Nebuchadnezzar"—now that is an interesting thought. I could see Paul being called God's
servant and Joseph as God's servant, but the wicked and cruel
King Nebuchadnezzar? We see that all of God's creation can
be used as His servants to do His bidding at any time He
desires. Yes, we are all tools in the hands of God, to be used
by Him for His purposes. Not everyone God uses signed up
for the job. Some servants serve without even knowing it.
Such was the case with King Nebuchadnezzar.

God used this cruel and evil king to bring about the
refining and building up of Daniel as well as the other three
Hebrew children. Throughout the Bible we will see that
when God's children, the Israelites, were not obedient, He
sent their enemies to chase them back to Himself. Even
our enemies can be used by God when we are not walking

uprightly before Him. Not only can God use our enemies to bring us back to Him, but they can also be used by God to help bring us to the different levels that He has destined for our lives.

Let's look back again at the life of Daniel. It was through King Nebuchadnezzar that Daniel was trained, disciplined, and promoted to be governor in a very hostile land. We must never think that God can only work through Christians or godly leadership alone. Even Satan himself is merely a screwdriver in the hand of God who is used to accomplish His purposes and desires in our lives. Keep in mind God would like to use godly leadership and mentors whenever possible. However, in the fallen world we live in, they are not always in the proper place or available to do His bidding.

All the resources of the world belong to God no matter who may seem to own them here on earth.

When it comes to making us into the people God desires us to be, no resources are off limits. Abraham grew up in the home of an idol maker. Yet, he became the father of our faith. Joseph received much of his education in the house of the Egyptian leader, Potiphar. God used him to save the known world and all the tribes of Israel from extinction by famine. Finally, look at the life of Moses. God used the household of Pharaoh, the very man who wanted Moses dead, to raise him and pay for the finest education for him. As we know, after all the work to train Moses, God used him to deliver the Israelites from the bondage of his Egyptian educators.

All the resources of the world belong to God—no matter who may seem to own them here on earth. God does not only work through Sunday school teachers or preachers, but whomever He may choose to help bring about His plan. Not everyone God uses to build His kingdom will see it. Not everyone who is helping accomplish God's will even knows they are being used. No earthly resource is off limits in bringing about the will of God in our lives.

Do you feel like your boss is more like Attila the Hun than Mother Teresa? Be of good cheer—God can use him. Are you being trained in an ungodly atmosphere? Fear not—God can keep you. The Bible shows us that sometimes God uses His choicest servants in the most hostile arenas. All God wants is your permission to be used and He will do the rest.

WEEK 6

HALF-TRUTHS OR WHOLE LIES

**Then Abimelech called Abraham, and said
unto him, What hast thou done unto us? and what
have I offended thee, that thou hast brought on
me and on my kingdom a great sin? thou has
done deeds unto me that ought not to be done.**

**And Abimlech said unto Abraham, What
sawest thou, that thou has done this thing?**

**And Abraham said, Because I thought,
Surely the fear of God is not in this place;
and they will slay me for my wife's sake.**

**And yet indeed she is my sister; she is the
daughter of my father, but not the daughter
of my mother; and she became my wife.**

Genesis 20:9-12 (KJV)

When is a half-truth not the truth? It is not the truth
when it is a whole lie. Here we see Abraham, the
father of our faith, being called on the carpet by King
Abimelech for telling the king that Sarah, his wife, was his
sister. God had just warned the king in a dream that if he so
much as touched a hair on her head he would surely die. I
think it is quite wonderful how God does not hesitate to
reveal the sins and weaknesses of even His greatest servants.
The Bible is filled with examples of how each one of His

servants have failed Him at one time or another. Abraham goes on to explain that Sarah really is his half sister and so in reality he was telling the truth...*Not!* There are a few things we want to look at here when it comes to telling the truth.

The first thing we see is that *half* a truth can get you in a *whole* lot of trouble. If the king had slept with Sarah, the mother of Israel would have been severely tainted. It also would have caused all the women in King Abimelech's family to be barren, which would bring an end to his family line—all of this because Abraham told *half the truth*. Half-truths are very deadly because people tend to believe they are doing the right thing based on the assumption that since half of the information is true, the other half is true also. However, if we build on any foundation other than total truth, whatever is built will be sure to fall.

Whatever is achieved by deception will not stand the test of time.

The reason Abraham feared telling the truth is he feared for his life. Whenever we do anything with fear as a foundation, it will always be doomed to fail. Whenever we set out to save our lives, we are sure to lose them. Very often people fail to tell the truth because of the fear of man. The Bible is clear that **"the fear of man brings a snare..." (Proverbs 29:25 NAS)**. By the way, man pleasing is a close cousin of the fear of man. As a people of faith we are to set our sights on pleasing God and Him alone. Once we have decided to please God and not fear what man can do to us, then, and only then, are we in a safe place. Remember, **"For God has not given us a spirit of fear, but of power and of love and of a sound mind" (II Timothy 1:7 NKJV)**.

The next time you are tempted to deceive by telling a half–truth, examine your motive. In most cases, the fear of man has something to do with it. Remember that whatever is achieved by deception will not stand the test of time. God loves you too much to let you succeed in a lie. Sooner or later your foundation will crumble and you will have to build again. It is much wiser to speak the truth and let God deal with the consequences. God is a God of truth and He has promised to bless the truth.

WEEK 7

GET LOST

He that findeth his life shall lose it: and he that loseth his life for my sake shall find it.
Matthew 10:39 (KJV)

People spend great amounts of money and effort trying to find themselves. I have been spending my whole life trying to do the opposite. Think about it—if you ever do find yourself, what are you going to find? You find what you should be trying to lose…a sinner in desperate need of a Savior. The Scripture above says it all. If we try to *find* our life, we will lose it. Our whole mission in life should be to find Jesus and when we do, make sure we hold on tight.

Our culture keeps telling us life is all about us. Every commercial on television puts the focus on us. We must lose weight; our breath must smell good; we must look good; and the beat goes on. There is an epidemic of eating disorders among teenage girls because they believe they must look a certain way to be loved and accepted by society, especially by teenage boys. The quickest and simplest way to find peace in today's world is to lose its standards and find Christ's standards.

What are Christ's standards? You have probably heard about how hard it is to serve God and meet His standards. I am not going to say that serving God is easy because that certainly would be misleading. However do not be deceived.

Serving Satan and this world system is not only hard but also fruitless. Serving Satan gives you nothing but misery here, which is just to get you ready for the misery that lies ahead. The wonderful thing about trying to meet Christ's standards is that He gives us the ability to do it. It is like taking a test, and just as you are about to begin, the teacher hands you the answer key. Jesus is the Answer to every trial and difficulty we will have in this life. He will also walk through each situation with us.

When we make knowing Him the object of our desire, all other desires fade away.

When we begin to lay down our desires and tell God we want His desires to be ours, this is the beginning of new life. The truth is, you do not have to satisfy any of your desires when He becomes your desire. When we make knowing Him the object of our desire, all other desires fade away in His wonderful presence. Hence, if we try to lose our life we will find it.

How sad it is that so many of the people we know and love have wasted so much of their lives looking for that which cannot give life. Begin today on a journey to know Jesus like never before. Make finding and knowing Him your prized possession. I promise that only His love and favor will bring relief from the exhausting and fruitless process of trying to find yourself.

WEEK 8

FORBIDDEN FRUIT

And when the woman saw that the tree was good for food, and that is was pleasant to the eyes, and a tree to be desired to make one wise, she took of the fruit thereof, and did eat, and gave also to unto her husband with her; and he did eat.

Genesis 3:6 (KJV)

In the above Scripture, we have a bird's-eye view into the fall of man. It starts with an unsolicited conversation with the enemy of our soul, Satan, and the first lady, Eve. Somehow this odd couple begins a conversation in the Garden discussing the things of God. Well, at least that is what he would like her to believe. After their conversation, Eve looks at the Tree of Knowledge and this time she notices how pleasant it is to her eyes and decides to go and eat of it. This, my friend, was the beginning of all sorrows.

Immediately after Eve ate of the fruit God had forbidden her to eat, she goes on to give Adam a bite. Without questioning anything Eve is doing, Adam also partakes of the forbidden fruit and becomes an accessory to the crime. The Bible states, **"and the eyes of them both were opened and they knew that they were naked…"** (Genesis 3:7 KJV). They then took some fig leaves and sewed them together to cover themselves up. We have just witnessed the first cover-up in human history. They covered themselves up because for the first time since creation, they had lost their innocence and realized just how weak and vulnerable they really were.

God had clearly told Adam and Eve not to eat of the fruit of that tree, not because He was trying to keep something from them, but because there were things in life God knew they just did not need to know.

There are things that as a loving Father He is trying to protect us from. In the case of Adam and Eve, it was their rebellious nature. The same is true for us. Because God has given us all a free will, it is up to us to choose to trust God or do what we see as good.

What we sow in sin we will reap in temptation.

One good friend of mine put it this way—what we sow in sin we will reap in temptation. If we never knew how good a chocolate fudge sundae tasted, we would never have to fight the desire to have one. In other words, once we have the taste of something in our lives, it is extremely difficult to lose that taste. No one tries cocaine for the first time thinking this is the beginning of a lifelong battle with addiction, but very often it is. God warns us to stay away from certain things for the simple reason that He does not want us having to wrestle with these sins and temptations for the rest of our lives. This is why to the pure all things are pure. They do not have these dark histories they must battle.

My friend, trust that whatever it is God has asked you to stay away from is not to control or manipulate your life, but so you would have life and have it more abundantly (see John 10:10). It is so you can spend your time pursuing Him and not fighting the devils and consequences of your past life. Remember God will forgive all your sins, but you must still deal with the memories, scars, and consequences they leave behind. The world has never been the same since Adam and Eve ate the forbidden fruit. So it will be with you. You can choose to eat the forbidden fruit or choose to obey God.

WEEK 9

AND THEY WATCHED HIM

And the scribes and Pharisees watched him, whether he would heal on the sabbath day; that they might find an accusation against him.

Luke 6:7 (KJV)

We are a watched people. Whether it is at work, home, in church, or the mall, someone is always looking. Whether it is God or the enemy, friend or foe, someone is checking to see if you really are who you say you are. Jesus also lived under constant scrutiny. Just the mention of His name would draw a crowd. The sad thing is, often people did not come to honor Him but to criticize Him and find fault. More and more each day we are faced with the issue of living transparent lives. So we must ask ourselves, "If we were put on trial for being a Christian, a husband, a mother, or a friend, would they have enough evidence to convict us?"

Here are some tips from the life of Jesus that will help us to live consistent lives in a world filled with inconsistencies. Although Jesus knew people were watching every move He made, this never intimidated Him. In fact, He used their watchfulness as an opportunity to speak truth into their lives. The reason He was not intimidated by their scrutiny was He did not have any hidden agendas. His only mission in life was to bless and bring hope to those hopelessly bound in sin. With Jesus, the truth was always in fashion. It did not matter who was watching or who was asking questions. He always gave them the same response—the truth that could set them free.

Simply put, the key to a transparent life is a pure heart. Jesus' only desire was to carry out the will of His Father. He was not reactive but proactive. Many times in life we find ourselves in trouble because we do not have what I will call here a mission statement. We take life as it comes instead of following the blueprint laid out for us by God the Creator. When we are not proactive and do not know what we are called to accomplish in a situation, we often react wrongly to people who question our motives or behavior. That is why Jesus could always respond in love to those who would question Him. He knew that whatever He was doing was meant to bring truth and freedom to those very people questioning Him.

He used their watchfulness as an opportunity to speak truth into their lives.

It is funny that although Jesus preached a hard-line on sin, sinners loved Him. They always wanted to be around Him. Why? Because He was real and He showed love. He lived what He preached and most importantly He had their best interest at heart. Who would not want to be around a man who just wanted to bless and bring hope to everyone He crossed paths with? Jesus' holiness attracted them because He did not use it as a weapon against them, but as an advertisement for how good life can be.

The world is hungry for the real thing. They are tired of deceiving and being deceived. They are tired of living with the fruit of their lies and deception. They have heard the church talk of a better way, but have never seen it come to pass. They hunger to see if there are men and women who are real and transparent, and who can point to a better way while still being able to admit their failures. There is real freedom in being real. Living a double life can be very confusing and very fruitless. The challenge today is to be real. You will be surprised to see that people do not need to see perfection in you, only truth spoken in love.

WEEK 10

AND NOAH BUILT AN ALTAR

And Noah builded an altar unto the Lord; and took of every clean beast, and of every clean fowl, and offered burnt offerings on the altar.

Genesis 8:20 (KJV)

Here is something that might come as a shock to some people. The rebuilding of the world, as we know it, began around an altar. After God destroyed the world with forty days and forty nights of rain, the first thing Noah did after emerging from the ark was to build an altar where he could bring a sacrifice to worship God. I do not know about you, but to me that is a very significant thing.

First, we know that the altar of God is a holy place. In the Old Testament days it was a place where sacrifice was brought and made to God on behalf of sinful man—a place of both death and worship. Now there is an interesting combination. You see, from the beginning God required that death be a part of worship. In Old Testament days, it was the death of some type of animal. Remember God would not accept Cain's sacrifice because it did not contain the blood of any living thing. Today it is still about death and blood. It is about dying to the things of this world and accepting the death and the shed blood of His holy Son, Jesus, as a covering for our sins. This is what allows us to enter into the holy place and be at peace with God.

Look around and we will see that we live in a culture that idolizes life and the young. Yet there is something very important that we must see here in this passage. God saw fit to make the altar (a place of death), to be the starting place of life. Jesus put it this way, unless a seed falls into the ground and dies, it cannot bring forth life (see John 12:24). In other words, true life can only be found when we die to the things of this world and grasp onto those things of eternal value.

The altar was not only meant to be a place of death, but a place where we could find newness of life.

Today the altar is not only a place to lay down our will and ways, but also a place to give our hearts to Jesus and walk away with a living relationship with the Creator of the universe. You see, the altar was not only meant to be a place of death, but a place where we could find newness of life.

Noah knew that before doing anything else, he must build an altar where he could continue to worship his Creator and his God. In the days of Noah, an altar was usually nothing more than a pile of rocks. But make no mistake about it, that pile of rocks had great meaning. As we close, let me encourage you to find an altar, a place where you get alone with God, a place where you can die to your will and find His. One thing has not changed, worship still involves death, and only through dying to ourselves and to the things of this world will we find real life.

WEEK 11

TRUE OR TRUTH

**Jesus said to him, "I am the way,
the truth, and the life. No one comes
to the Father except through Me."
John 14:6 (NKJV)**

You may be thinking, "Preacher, are you splitting hairs? Aren't true and truth the same thing?" Believe it or not, there is a difference. Although truth will always be true, not everything that is true is truth. For instance, today it might be true that you have enough money in the bank to pay your bills. However, if the bank makes an error and returns one of your checks, your true statement can be made false. Many people will go to the doctor feeling perfectly healthy, only to find out there is a dreaded disease lurking in their body. Yes, it was true they were feeling healthy, but the truth was they were not healthy at all.

So what are some of the differences between a true statement and a truth statement? First, a truth statement is eternal. It never changes. Only God can speak truth. The only time man can speak the truth is when he is repeating what God has already said. On the other hand, true statements change all the time. True statements change with time and circumstance. At fourteen years old a child may be five feet tall. At sixteen they may be six feet tall. They were both true at different times of their lives. The truth is the child will never grow one inch past what God has put in their DNA. Are you beginning to see that it is more important to know the truth about a matter than to know what may be true at the time?

In our world of chronos time, our true statements may one day all be false. In God's world of kairos time, truth rings eternal. Jesus said, **"I am the way, the *truth*, and the life (John 14:6).** When He said He was the truth, it meant His words would always be truth. This is one of the unchanging characteristics of God. He is the same yesterday, today, and forever (see Hebrews 13:8). What He said two thousand years ago still works today. His principles are timeless. They will work in any country, on any day, and for any person who chooses to believe them and walk by faith.

> *Although truth will always be true, not everything that is true is truth.*

Even when a person puts their hand on a Bible in court and swears to tell the whole truth, they are only telling what they saw or heard with their limited vision, hearing, and understanding. Truth, on the other hand, does not need to have someone to bear witness to it for it to be truth. Truth gets its credibility from the Creator. Because God created all things, He alone knows the truth about all things. Because God sees all things not just externally but also internally, looking into the heart of a matter, He is able to speak truth. This is why God tells us not to judge a man. To bring true judgment, you must have total truth. Without the help of God we are unable to have total truth on a matter because of our limited senses and understanding.

So the next time you are talking to someone and you start to say, "To tell you the truth...," stop and think about it. Perhaps it would be better said, "The truth as I understand it is." That would be a much more accurate statement. In reality, quoting the Word of God is the closest we will ever get to speaking the truth.

WEEK 12

THE FATHERLESS CHURCH

**I am not writing this to shame you,
but to warn you, as my dear children.**

**Even though you have ten thousand guardians in
Christ, you do not have many fathers, for in Christ
Jesus I became your father through the gospel.**

Therefore, I urge you to imitate me.

I Corinthians 4:14-16

The twentieth century church has come a long way from the New Testament church of old. But unfortunately, in many ways this has not necessarily been a good thing. While in some areas the church may have seen some slight improvement, it has remained difficult to better that which came first.

In my opinion, no area has seen less improvement than the area of "fathering" in the church. We have gone from a church built on the early fathers to an orphanage in search of a father. Today's church hires men to be pastors as opposed to churches gathered and started by men who are fathers. In this passage, Paul warned that although there were many teachers available to the church at Corinth, he was still their father. Men can be trained to preach or teach, but it takes the father heart of God in a person to be a father.

However, like a child who might go through fifteen or more teachers before he graduates from high school, he still only has one father.

So why did Paul warn the church at Corinth about the importance of recognizing him as their spiritual father? First, it is important that we see there are some men called to be spiritual fathers in the Lord to the newborn in the Spirit. Second, we must see that there are some major differences between fathers in the Lord and teachers. Let's briefly look at some of these differences and what might have caused Paul to be concerned.

A father's heart is not just to teach, but to impart himself into his children.

As Paul mentioned in verse sixteen, teachers of the Word are plentiful. This is not to knock any of those gifted of God who are called to rightly divide the word of truth. However, a father's heart is not just to teach, but to impart himself into his children. Hence, it is in the kingdom that a spiritual father will literally give of himself, not just teach the Word in raising up spiritual children. Like Paul, he will not fear to say, **"Follow my example, as I follow the example of Christ" (I Corinthians 11:1).** These men have the confidence to say this not because they think they are flawless or sinless. Rather, they feel the God-given responsibility to make sure that their spiritual children do not just learn the Word, but mature in the Word and become mothers and fathers themselves. What good, earthly parent does not raise their children to one day leave the house and become parents themselves? Why should it not be the same in the kingdom? We should not be looking to increase church membership, but rather, to raise up godly sons and daughters in the Spirit.

Second, spiritual fathers are not just thinking of the people in front of them at the moment, but how those people will impact future generations. In the natural, you become a father, then a grandfather, and so on. Grandchildren are always on the mind of good, loving parents. Equally, Paul's concern was not just for the church at Corinth, but for the example they would set for other churches to come in the future.

Teachers will come and go because they do not carry the same burdens of a father. Teachers primarily carry the burden to study the Word of God and then share their findings with God's people. Fathers on the other hand have a totally different burden—to raise up and release. They are not quick to move away from their children. They will keep teaching and imparting all that they have, both in the natural and in the spiritual, until they feel their children are ready to successfully stand on their own.

Simply put, although a father teaches, it is his love that makes the biggest difference in the life of his child. By the way, is it not wonderful to know that this is the same love that God has toward us? He is not just interested in our gaining knowledge, but our becoming just like Him. Thank God for spiritual fathers who answer the call of God to help in this great undertaking.

WEEK 13

ORIGINAL SIN?

Wherefore, as by one man sin entered into the world, and death by sin; and so death passed upon all men, for that all have sinned.
Romans 5:12 (KJV)

I have heard sin called many things, but I never quite thought of it as original. This actually is a term theologians use to denote the fact that all humans are born into sin and that all sin began with Adam and Eve, the mother and father of humanity. The truth is, our sins are very much the same as those of our fathers and forefathers. No matter what our weaknesses are and what type of sins we commit, it always comes down to the same thing—saying yes to our flesh and saying no to God's will and His Word. Only one Man has been able to stand up to sin and have a perfect record—Jesus, the Son of Man and the Son of God.

So why is it so hard to have victory over the same sin? If you knew exactly where the bear trap was in the woods you would never walk into it, right? How is it then that people keep walking into the same old sins? Here are a few thoughts on how to avoid those "same old" sins that seem to be a part of our lives.

God has promised to deliver us from our enemies, not our friends. Too often these pet sins become like old friends. They make occasional visits, stay a while, and then leave only to come back again when least expected. We must declare war on that which is not of God. If it is His enemy, it must be our enemy. Sin must not find a welcome mat at the door of our hearts.

Second, knowledge is not necessarily power. Just because we know something is sin does not mean we have the power to resist or overcome it. If knowledge were power, the Pharisees would have been mighty men of God. They were the most learned men of their times, but Jesus called them whitewashed tombs (see Matthew 23:27). They looked good on the outside but on the inside they were dead. *Information does not mean transformation.* We must submit our knowledge to God and humbly ask Him for the power to overcome that which we know is wrong. "**...You do not have, because you do not ask God**" **(James 4:2).**

God has promised to deliver us from our enemies, not our friends.

Finally, change must begin in the heart. Changing our behavior or environment will only work for so long. All sin begins in the heart. Whatever has our hearts has our lives. This is why Jesus said we must "**...love the Lord your God with all your heart...**" **(Matthew 22:37).** Jesus also said, "**...where your treasure is, there your heart will be also**" **(Matthew 6:21).** So here it is—we should put our treasure where we want our hearts to follow. This will be the beginning of a new walk with Him and that will bring new victory over original sin!

WEEK 14

GROWN-UPS?

And they brought young children to him, that he should touch them: and his disciples rebuked those that brought them.

But when Jesus saw it, he was much displeased, and said unto them, Suffer the little children to come unto me, and forbid them not: for of such is the kingdom of God.

Mark 10:13-14 (KJV)

So who says *"I'm* a grown-up?" I'm forty-nine and I still do not like liver and I still like to play with toys. Admittedly, my toys are bigger and a little more expensive, but that's another story. You have probably heard it said or have said it to your children, "If you get lost or get in trouble, look for a grown-up." Well, I hate to break it you, but most grown-ups are still a little lost and some are in a lot of trouble. Many times we reach adulthood, but not maturity. It is important as we get older that we do not become hardened by the hard knocks of life. This is what Jesus loved about children, their tender hearts.

Let me destroy a few more myths. Getting old is no guarantee we are getting wiser. Unfortunately, not everyone with white hair is wise, and sin does not stop chasing us after we hit fifty. Actually, we never stop growing up unless we choose to. Graduating from high school or college is not a signal to stop learning or turn off our minds. They are just stones of remembrance to let us know where we have been and in what direction we are heading. Actually, Jesus said **"...unless you change and become like little children, you will never enter the kingdom of heaven" (Matthew 18:3).** Here is something to think about: The only people who have to become like little children are grown-ups. Another way of putting this is that we have to learn how to grow down. The older we get the more we have to strive to keep the spirit, innocence, and simplicity of a child.

A few characteristics of a child that I believe bless the heart of God are as follows. Children are born totally dependent on their parents. At the beginning of their lives they are pure and innocent, not questioning those in authority. They love and trust their parents and give them great joy. Their hearts are very tender and can give and receive love freely. They are also teachable.

Getting old is no guarantee you are getting wiser.

We can see now why Jesus wants us to become like children, who for the most part are dependent, submissive, loving, trusting, and teachable. These are the very qualities most of us lose as we grow up and the very qualities we love about our children when they are young. They are also the very qualities that God wants us to strive to hold onto throughout our lives. I think I would rather be known as a *growing up* rather than a grown-up. At least then I will always have a little room to improve or mature.

WEEK 15

CRAZY PRAISE

Upon receiving such orders, he put them in the inner cell and fastened their feet in the stocks. About midnight Paul and Silas were praying and singing hymns to God, and the other prisoners were listening to them.
Acts 16:24-25

There are times when it seems crazy to praise the Lord. More than anyone in the Bible, David understood the power of praise. Praise is mentioned more than one hundred fifty times in the book of Psalms. Much of the book of Psalms was written while David was going through some very deep waters in his life. Yet David said, **"Let everything that has breath praise the Lord" (Psalm 150:6).** This brings us to the heart of the matter—do we praise God only when it makes sense or *until* it makes sense?

If we look at the saints of the Bible, they praised God at some pretty obscure times. In Acts 16, we read about Paul and Silas praising the Lord while locked up in prison. What is interesting is that some people will say people who praise the Lord do not end up in prison. However, if you look in the Bible you will find God's servants praising and worshiping Him in all types of situations, sometimes very unusual situations. When all else has let us down, it is good to know we serve a God who is ever present and ready to move on our behalf whenever we begin to praise Him. Remember, the Bible does not say He inhabits our prayers or our prophecies, but our praises (see Psalm 22:3). That means when we praise Him, we bring Him into whatever situation we are facing and He brings us the victory.

Now, the reason we can praise God even when everything seems to be going wrong is that nothing really depends on us. When we walk in obedience, our lives are in His hands, and it is our responsibility to trust Him and His responsibility to work things out for our benefit. If we really believe Romans 8:28 which says **"...that all things work together for good..."** (KJV), we can give God praise at all times. Like Paul and Silas in prison, although they were physically bound, their hearts were free to praise their God, which brought them their physical freedom. Is it not funny that they were freer in jail than the jailor whose job it was to keep them there? Praise brings freedom to any situation because it brings the power of God into every situation.

> *When we praise Him, we bring Him into whatever situation we are facing and He brings us the victory.*

Today you may be facing some deep waters, perhaps sickness, marital problems, or financial reversals. Whatever you are facing, know that we serve a great God who is able to meet all of our needs. The down payment of our trust is our praise. The praise of our mouths is the best weapon against the fear of our hearts. Whether you are reading this book in a prison or in a church balcony, there is never a bad time to begin praising the Lord. Give Him a praise offering for what you need done in your life and watch Him meet your need in a way you never thought possible.

WEEK 16

TO EVERY THING A SEASON

**To every thing there is a season, and a
time to every purpose under the heaven.**
Ecclesiastes 3:1 (KJV)

Some of the most difficult times in our lives are times of transition. Times of transition are times when God is moving us from one level or place to another. The reason these times are so difficult is because as humans we tend to find our peace and security in our place, not His presence. However, if our holy God allowed us to live in the comfort of a lie, He would actually be less than holy.

God wants us to find our comfort and security in Him. People or places will not suffice. In the verse above, Solomon brings a timeless truth that every thing has a time, a place, and a season in our lives. Seasons come and go in our lives just like seasons come and go in our physical world. People leave us, people die, situations change, addresses change, and unfortunately, even marriage partners change. These are the seasons of life. Nothing stays the same. One of the surest ways to get depressed is to try and go back to a place in our lives that no longer exists. Life was meant to be lived forward; you cannot go back!

God has made our lives to be an adventure of walking with Him, not without Him. This is why our life in Him is called a Christian "walk," not a Christian stay. This is also why in Matthew 17, when Jesus was on the Mount and was transfigured before His disciples, they wanted to build tabernacles and stay for a while. After all, what a beautiful place to be! They had found their security in a place, not in Jesus. Notice that He did not let them stay there. Notice also that as they were making their way down the mountain, the first thing they ran into was the demon-possessed boy. So much for peaceful surroundings!

God wants to teach you to enjoy the process, not the destination.

If our security is not in the Prince of Peace, do not count on it being around for too long. Our security must be in the fact that no matter what the season, He is always there, not that we are always in that season. The truth is that whatever season we are in right now, whether it is good or bad, it will probably have little effect on us a year from now. Today we might be walking through deep waters that feel like they are about to overflow us. They will not. They will just float you to the new level God wants to bring you to.

When the Israelites were about to cross over the Red Sea, they were murmuring and complaining. They had the Red Sea in front of them and the enemy behind them—not a pretty picture. However, notice the first thing they did after they crossed. They basically had a party and praised God for His deliverance. That is how fast their season changed. That is also how fast God can do it for you!

Paul said, **"I know both how to be abased, and I know how to abound..." (Philippians 4:12 KJV).** He had seen both seasons. The truth of the matter is not how much you are enjoying the season you are in, but learning how to be content in all seasons because it is all part of the big plan for your life. Understanding seasons is very important to the growth and happiness of your life in Christ. You do not go looking for snow in the summer. If you do, you will be disappointed every time. Learn to understand the seasons of your lives. *God wants to teach you to enjoy the process, not the destination.* Today, find God in your season. Do not just hope for a new season. Pray you can find the things you need in this one. The secret of a life of growth is to find peace and joy in every season. When you find God where you are, that is when God will usually take you to the next place!

WEEK 17

TEACH US
TO PRAY

**One day Jesus was praying in a certain place.
When he finished, one of his disciples
said to him, "Lord, teach us to pray,
just as John taught his disciples."**

Luke 11:1

I am convinced that when the disciples heard Jesus pray, they realized they did not know how to pray. After all the time they had spent with the Master, they were just realizing this important fact. In our society today, there are so many books and teachings on prayer that we would think everyone would know how to pray. However, just like the disciples, I fear we also must say, **"Lord, teach us to pray."**

One of the first things we see modeled in Jesus' life is that He had a strong desire to get alone with God for the purpose of communion. He would hide away in the mountains, out on the water, or in the countryside just to be alone with God. One of the main reasons Jesus sought God out in prayer was because He realized that only through fervent prayer could the kingdom of God be established. It is not organizations, programs, or even discipline that moves the hand of God— it is prayer. James puts it this way: **"The effectual fervent prayer of a righteous man availeth much" (James 5:16 KJV).** Simply put, prayer moves God.

So if Jesus thought so much of prayer that He constantly made time to be alone with God, why is it that so many of us have a hard time making it an important part of our lives? Amazingly enough, I believe the number one reason people do not make time to pray is not that Christians are lazy or sinful, but rather that they really do not believe it will make a difference. Satan has many people believing that prayer is a waste of time, and in the long run it will not change anything. This is perhaps one of Satan's greatest accomplishments—to rob the saints of their very life source, communication with God.

Prayer is not natural, but it will bring the supernatural.

John 15 clearly teaches us that unless we are connected into the vine we can do nothing (see John 15:5). To bear fruit that will last, to make a difference in our world, prayer is most necessary. Prayer will not only bring God's power and wisdom into the situation you are dealing with, but it will also bring great change to the attitude you have toward that situation. Prayer shows us the big picture. It shows us what really counts. When Jesus was in the Garden of Gethsemane praying for the cup to be lifted from Him, it did not change God's plan, but it did change Jesus' attitude toward the plan. Once God showed Him the importance of what He was to do, He never wavered from that point forward (see Matthew 26:39-42).

Are you struggling with something that God has told you to do or facing a hard time in your life? Maybe it is because you need to see the big picture. The best place to find God's will is in His Word. The best place to get the strength to carry it out is in prayer. This is why the disciples needed to pray. After spending three years traveling and living with

Jesus, they had plenty of knowledge. What they needed was the strength to carry out effectively what they already knew. This is where prayer comes in. Prayer is not easy but necessary. Prayer is not natural, but it will bring the supernatural. Finally, prayer can seem like work but it will bring the grace to carry out God's work.

WEEK 18

SEPARATION OF CHURCH AND STATE

Hazael went to meet Elisha, taking with him as a gift forty camel-loads of all the finest wares of Damascus. He went in and stood before him, and said, "Your son Ben-Hadad king of Aram has sent me to ask, 'Will I recover from this illness?'"

Then Hazael left Elisha and returned to his master. When Ben-Hadad asked, "What did Elisha say to you?" Hazael replied, "He told me that you would certainly recover."

II Kings 8:9, 14

The separation of church and state has become a very controversial issue in our country. It may also come as a surprise to some that this idea did not come about from some amendment written in the Constitution of the United States of America. The way this amendment is interpreted today is that the church is to have no influence in matters pertaining to government or public affairs. After all, what does the church or the Bible know about how to govern people? We will find, however, that God has a very different reason for keeping the church separated from the state.

In the passage listed, Ben-Hadad, the king, was very sick and needed a little reassurance from the man of God as to the future of his life. There are a few things we want to take note of here. First of all, we see that separation of church and state is a very old issue. Second, we see that God and not the government instituted it. There were kings and there were prophets. It was appropriate, even necessary at times, for the prophet to get involved in the king's business, but God help the king who tried to get involved in the prophet's business. Kings greeted prophets much the way commoners greeted kings, bearing many gifts—especially if they wanted a good word from God. In God's economy, separation of church and state meant that the state should stay out of the church's business. However, He meant for the church to be invited into the state's business.

The church will not suffer by the state staying out of their affairs. The same cannot be said for the opposite situation.

In the Old Testament, the only way God communicated with kings, or anyone for that matter, was through His servants the prophets. Different kings would work with different prophets to bring about the will of God on the earth. God designed it so the kings would always be in need of prophets in order for them to know what God's plans were for future events. God knew if He allowed kings to talk directly to Him, it would be way too much power to give to one man or government. It would also do away with the office of the prophet and the influence of His kingdom on the earth. So God's policy was that if a king needed to know what God thought about a situation, he had to humble himself and go seek out the prophet. God saw to it that a prophet was always necessary and available to deliver the word of the Lord to the kings and leaders who needed to communicate with Him and find out His will.

It was the prophet Samuel who anointed David to be king. It was the prophet Nathan who revealed to King David his sin with Bathsheba. It was the prophet Isaiah who brought King Hezekiah the bad news that his death would be coming soon. After King Hezekiah prayed and asked God for an extension on his life, God answered the prayer by granting him a fifteen-year extension. God did not answer King Hezekiah directly; He sent Isaiah back with the good news.

Today, the argument for the separation between church and state continues to rage on. Politicians claim the church can have no voice in the state. To their credit they have also tried to stay out of the affairs of the church. The truth is that the church will not suffer by the state staying out of their affairs. The same cannot be said for the opposite situation. Without the church bringing biblical values and morality to the nation, it will suffer tremendously. We already are paying the price for the many humanistic ways we think and behave. It is my prayer that one day the church will walk in such great power and love that it will become attractive to the world and our influence will be desired and not required.

WEEK 19

BURIED TREASURE

When I saw in the plunder a beautiful robe from Babylonia, two hundred shekels of silver and a wedge of gold weighing fifty shekels, I coveted them and took them. They are hidden in the ground inside my tent, with the silver underneath.

Joshua 7:21

Some treasures we bury—some end up burying us. This is the story of Achan. Achan was a soldier on the winning side, a husband, a father, and unfortunately, a thief. It was the last title that buried him. Joshua had clearly stated that certain spoils of the victory at Jericho were to be set apart for the Lord. It was made very clear that anyone touching these devoted things would bring destruction to their lives. Isn't it always the forbidden fruit that causes the greatest temptation? Like Judas, Achan had a problem with things— they owned him instead of him having ownership over them. We have two main lessons we can learn from this.

First, we see that a lust for things is every bit as dangerous as sexual lust for a man or a woman. The church talks much about sexual sin and lust, but the Bible says that it is the **"love of money" (I Timothy 6:10)** that is the root of all evil. Isn't it funny that in a capitalistic society such as ours, sins that involve money do not get much press? Yet, we may make the argument from this passage that it is evil.

Now here is an interesting question: What do Judas, Ananias, Sapphira, and Achan all have in common? They all had a problem with materialism until they all lost their lives and the possessions they thought were so important. By comparison, God was much more gracious to Rahab, the harlot, and the prostitute woman at the well.

I am not trying to make a theology out of this; I am only trying to show that greed and coveting that which is not ours are dangerous sins. In addition, if these sins are not dealt with and repented of, they can lead to death. To put it simply, coveting is a desire for those things that God has not given you. Perhaps God has even clearly told you that you cannot have them. In Achan's case, the desire turned to the actual taking of those things. Although sexual sins get much more attention in the church today, God does not overlook these sometimes more socially acceptable sins. It may even come as a surprise to some that two of the Ten Commandments have to do with possessions while only one has to do with sex (see Exodus 20). From this little fact, one could make the argument that it is twice as easy to sin when it comes to materialism as it is to sin sexually.

Sin is infectious! If you will keep it out of your heart, it can never get into your house.

One of the great benefits of the tithe is to keep this deadly desire to idolize possessions under control. As we regularly give ten percent of our money to the Lord (for those who may not know, that is what it means to tithe), we are helping to break the back of greed and covetousness in our lives. Also, keep in mind that God clearly states the tithe is holy and belongs to Him. Therefore, to hold on to what belongs to Him is stealing and worse yet, stealing from God (see Malachi 3:8-12).

The point here is that whether it is sexual sin, greed, or pride, no one sins alone. Although Achan seemed to have sinned alone (we have no real record that his family took part in his sin), they paid the price along with him. Because of his unrestrained lust for things, his whole family paid the ultimate price. The sins of our lives are carried into the lives of those we love. Our weaknesses and shortcomings have a devastating effect on those we love. The alcoholic who never seems to make it home with his check brings great pain and shame to his family. *He may drink alone, but he does not sin alone.*

What are you bringing into your house and what effect might it have on your children and loved ones? I am sure Achan never intended to involve his family in his sin, but as we see they helped pay the price. All of Achan's family were destroyed because of disobedience and an uncontrolled desire for things. Sin is infectious! If you will keep it out of your heart, it can never get into your house.

WEEK 20

W.U.S.H.

But they that wait upon the LORD shall renew their strength; they shall mount up with wings as eagles; they shall run, and not be weary; and they shall walk, and not faint.

Isaiah 40:31 (KJV)

Wait Until Something Happens. Wait. This word strikes fear in the heart of even God's choicest servants. In the instant-on world we live in that promises instant gratification for almost all of our wants and desires, the word "wait" is becoming almost obsolete in our vocabulary. We are willing to wait for some things, but want others to happen immediately. For example, doctors have waiting rooms, but when we are sick we never say, "I'm not going to the doctor because I don't want to have to wait." However, we get frustrated with God as we wait on Him to bring order from chaos and bring about perfection in us while living in a fallen world. If you look through the Bible, you will see some of God's greatest servants make some grievous mistakes by not waiting on God to fulfill His promises.

Remember Abraham, the father of our faith? God told him he would be the father of many nations. Approximately twelve years later with no baby in sight, he decided he would help God. With the blessing of his wife, whose faith was also wearing thin, Abraham slept with her handmaiden, Hagar, who gave him his firstborn, but not promised, son Ishmael (see Genesis 16). The fallout from that decision has still not ended. Abraham was a victim of not waiting.

Think about Aaron, the high priest brother of Moses. Moses was called up to Mount Sinai and left the most obvious person in charge—his brother, the high priest. While Moses was up on the mountain receiving the Ten Commandments and other vital instructions from God, things began to go awry down below. It seems the children of Israel got tired of waiting for their leader to return so they asked Aaron if it would be okay if they could create and worship a golden calf. A short note of wisdom here, *if you can create it, you cannot worship it.* Aaron went along with the scheme, and needless to say, they were all quickly corrected. These were some of God's finest servants. They just got frustrated in the waiting process. You or I may not have even faired this well.

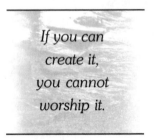

If you can create it, you cannot worship it.

What can we learn to help us wait with grace and faith? Perhaps the greatest thing we can learn about waiting is that we must learn to *wait on the Promiser, not the promise.* Waiting is a time to get to know more about the Father who gives us all good things. There is a reason for every delay. When we learn to trust God in all areas of our lives, we will see He can be trusted to keep His promises even when they seem to be late.

It is vital to understand the timing of God. Everything God does has a purpose and a time. If God promises you a baby, it is still going to take at least nine months. God does not work on our time schedule and He will not be rushed.

The longer it takes, the more time He is giving you to get to know Him. Do not keep looking for answers, but learn that every delay is an opportunity to become more intimate with the One who made the promise. Many times God has to wait on us until we are strong enough to hold onto the promise after receiving it.

Keep in mind even as you may be waiting on an answer from God, Satan is waiting also to steal the answer from you. It is during this waiting period we learn to have fellowship with God and get strength and wisdom to hold onto that which God has promised us. Perhaps you are waiting on something God has promised you. Although it may seem like He made that promise many moons ago, remember the answer is not the problem, learning to wait is.

WEEK 21

WAITING FOR A COMMAND

Then the Lord said to Moses, "Why are you crying out to me? Tell the Israelites to move on.

Raise your staff and stretch out your hand over the sea to divide the water so that the Israelites can go through the sea on dry ground."

Exodus 14:15-16

In one of our earlier writings we talked about the perils of waiting on God. Here we see quite a different situation. Moses seems to be waiting on God for the next move, and God basically says to him, "Hey what are you waiting for?" In the kingdom, waiting on God is half the challenge. Once God has given the command, however, it is then up to us to be obedient and carry out what God has spoken to complete the challenge. Waiting for more confirmation can sometimes be dangerous. On the other side of waiting on God is moving out in faith. When God speaks, we must move. It is a wonderful thing to be ready to wait on God, but remember God does not usually give all the instructions at once. He usually gives us enough to get started and then teaches us how to walk in daily obedience. When walking with God, the process is almost always as important as the destination (with the exception of heaven, of course).

We see here in this passage that God reproved Moses for not taking the authority that He had already given to him. Moses' rod was God's authority in his life. He had used it before with Pharaoh and he knew the power it represented. Moses' main problem was not his lack of faith as much as his willingness to listen to the complaining and fearfulness of the people. It is dangerous to let the voices of people drown out the voice of God. We must get alone with God to hear His voice. Throughout the gospels, we see Jesus walking away from the crowds at various times to get alone with His Father. Those who hear God will never lack a following. Jesus was a beautiful example of this. His goal was never to please man but to please His Father. In doing so, He never lacked a ministry or people to minister to.

> *Those who hear God will never lack a following.*

It would be safe to say that God does not like to repeat Himself when it comes to instructions. He also carefully watches our reaction to His instructions. Just ask Adam and Eve. They were given one chance to obey and when they disobeyed, there was no second chance, just discipline. Every obedience has its reward and every disobedience its consequence. We get to choose neither. Our only choice from the outset is to obey or not to obey.

When waiting on God for a command, keep in mind the three simple principles outlined in this passage. To begin with, be careful not to let the voices of those around you drown out the voice of God. As men and women of faith, our voice should be in tune to that of the Savior. **"The fear of man brings a snare" (Proverbs 29:25)**. This is not to say we should ignore the voices of God's people, but we must be careful not to confuse them. Second, realize the authority that God has already given to us. We sometimes wait for God to do things for us, which He already has given *us* the authority to do. We must always do our part if we expect God to do His.

Finally, note in Exodus 14:20, that God's presence, the cloud, provided light for the Israelites, but caused darkness for the Egyptians. There are times when we look at our enemies and get angry because outwardly they seem to be blessed, even more blessed than we may be. No amount of outward blessing can bring eternal life. It is only God's presence that brings true life to anything. What God uses for your salvation may turn out to be your enemy's destruction.

WEEK 22

WITH PERSECUTION

But he shall receive an hundredfold now in this time, houses, and brethren, and sisters, and mothers, and children, and lands, with persecutions; and in the world to come eternal life.

Mark 10:30 (KJV)

I cannot tell you how many times I have both heard and quoted the above Scripture and received a hundredfold return. It has been preached many times to people who probably had the wrong motive in giving, so therefore, they did not receive their hundredfold return. It is only recently that I somehow caught these two words that had been evading my eyes. It is truly amazing how they balance out the whole teaching on receiving a hundredfold return. Now I do not claim to have total understanding on this passage, but allow me to break it down with you and see if we can come to a better understanding of these very important Words.

In this passage, Jesus is responding to Peter's comment about having left all to follow Jesus (see Luke 18:28). Here we see the crux of the matter. There probably are not many people reading the above Scripture who have not at one time or another given money to the Lord while holding on to this Scripture of receiving a hundredfold return. I would venture to say many did not receive it—myself included, because we have never "left all." Now I am not saying there are not exceptions to this rule, or that the prosperity message as we have heard it does not work. However, I think this writing may add a little clarity to the message.

After hearing Peter's lament regarding having "left all," Jesus responded with this short teaching on giving. His main point was: If you have "left all" to follow after Christ, you will be provided for in every area that you gave up "all" (see Luke 18:29-30). If you left your house, you will find places to dwell. If you left your children, God will both take care of them and open your eyes to children you can invest some of your time and resources into. If you have left your family, you will find people who will greet you with open arms and find rich fellowship with them. It is also imperative that we are sent by God and do not just want to go. God only provides for those He sends—not those who want to go!

God only provides for those He sends— not those who want to go!

Let us stop here for a minute and examine one interesting thing. So often we hear teachings in the church about putting your family, especially your mate, first and above all else. Jesus made it clear here that some would be called, just like the disciples, to leave all. I will agree that this is probably a rare calling, but one certainly inside of God's will. Those people called by God to do this should receive much prayer support and encouragement from the church, not the condemnation that is so often the case.

Finally, He adds the clincher. Although we may be provided for, even abundantly, whoever goes out to do God's will, will encounter persecution. Whether it is a pastor in the local church or a missionary in a foreign land, persecution is part of the job description. All the blessings of God have a certain amount of persecution attached to them. We live in a fallen world where even the saints must deal with their fallen nature on a daily basis. When you give all, it is much easier to receive a hundredfold return. It really means you gave up your best to get God's best in return. It is not quite giving ten and getting back a thousand, but I believe it is still a great deal!

WEEK 23

"SIR, WE WOULD SEE JESUS"

**And there were certain Greeks among them
that came up to worship at the feast:**

**the same came therefore to Philip, which
was of Bethsaida of Galilee, and desired him,
saying, Sir, we would see Jesus.**

**Philip cometh and telleth Andrew:
and again Andrew and Philip tell Jesus.**

John 12:20-22 (KJV)

What a novel thought—going to church just to see Jesus. These Greek men had traveled to the temple for just that reason, to see Jesus. They had obviously heard about Him, His miracles, His power, and His love. No pomp, no circumstance, just, "Let me see Jesus." I wonder how we have become so sidetracked over the years? In many churches today Jesus has become a sideshow. You get to see Him after four offerings, twenty announcements, and three solos. Let's face it, church has become a lot more than just seeing Jesus.

Solos, offerings, and announcements are all part of a normal church service. I would even say most of the time they are necessary parts. The problem comes when we begin to love the church service so much that we leave without ever seeing Jesus. Jesus said, "If I be lifted up, I will draw all men nigh unto me" (see John 12:32). It is only the presence of God that will draw people to God. This is one of the main reasons we see so many churches struggling to grow. They have done everything to attract people and in doing so, have not attracted the Savior. It is a dangerous thing to leave God out of the equation.

In a society that idolizes being entertained, we must be careful that we do not go to church for the same reason. In many ways, our society has forced churches to become entertaining lest they become empty. However, no church that has the true presence of God will ever be empty. Entertainment is the counterfeit because He is the real thing. What people are truly searching for is a life touched by the presence of the Almighty. When God shows up at a place—whether it is a church, farm,

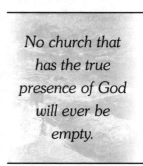

No church that has the true presence of God will ever be empty.

or an open field, you will not find people far behind. Earlier in this passage we read that people show up at the feast mainly because they heard Jesus was there. They had heard about how He raised Lazarus from the dead and performed other miracles.

Everywhere Jesus went He attracted crowds. He did not have to advertise or market Himself. In fact, many times He did His best to get away from crowds so He could spend time alone with His Father. Please understand, I am not saying that advertising or marketing is wrong; I am saying that if we have done all these things and cannot give the people Jesus, we have done it all in vain. We must make Him the main event. The whole meeting should be centered around the fact that Jesus will be present. So often people will travel hours to hear a speaker or a certain band when Jesus should be the main draw. The world has great speakers and great bands, but they do not have Jesus. They can market and advertise perhaps even better than the church, but they cannot produce Jesus. The church is the only institution that can introduce Jesus as the honored guest. Jesus lived and died to build His church.

Let us be reminded that the church has many wonderful programs and activities which have helped and blessed people for ages. This is not about picking on the church because we, the body of Christ, are the church. The church will be no more holy or Christ-centered than each individual is and desires to be. When it comes right down to it, we all must ask ourselves the same question: Are we going to church to be entertained, to take advantage of the good programs and good teachings, or is it to see Jesus? I have a feeling if we will go to church looking mainly to see Jesus, like the Greeks in the passage above, we will find Him. I appreciate the nice buildings and the programs and even the great worship, but, **"Sir, we would see Jesus."**

WEEK 24

AND THE SWORD SHALL NOT DEPART FROM THY HOUSE

Now, therefore, the sword will never depart from your house, because you despised me and took the wife of Uriah the Hittite to be your own.

II Samuel 12:10

It was not a good day for David. After almost a year of concealing his sin and thinking perhaps God had overlooked it, God finally sent Nathan the prophet to confront him. I believe if David would have confessed his sin to God voluntarily, things might have happened differently. However, he did not and it came down to the prophet of God having to bring the terrible news to David.

After carefully painting a picture to David of his own sin, and eventually bringing about what seemed like a true picture of David's heart regarding the matter, Nathan delivered the statement listed above that would change David's family forever. Even after David had confessed his sin and received God's forgiveness, his sin would forever be before him due to the consequences that even God would not change. This brings us to the main point of this writing.

Although God will forgive sins when we come to Him with a godly sorrow and heart of repentance, consequences last forever. I will admit there are times when God does seem to soften the road a bit for a repentant sinner. However, most times the consequences must be walked out. This was especially true here in the life of David.

We might also surmise from this story that those who know better from the beginning must especially walk out the consequences of their sins. David knew better. For a few moments of passion, David and his family paid an eternal price. For the rest of his life he saw turmoil in his family that very few since David have ever seen. This included the death of three of his children, the raping of a daughter, and the death of the first child he fathered with Bathsheba.

The fear of the Lord could save you a lifetime of regret.

Friends, Bathsheba comes in many forms. It may be a secret affair or a business deal done in secret that could cause the demise of your family. It may be a secret sin that has been nursed for years in the privacy of your heart. Remember God sees and knows all things; nothing is hidden from Him. I also find interesting what God said to David through the prophet Nathan. He said, "**...because you despised me...**" you committed this sin. Now I do not believe that this man whom God called a man after His own heart actually despised God, but when we know the Word of God and refuse to follow it, it is like a slap in the face to God. Like Joseph before him, David should have been running from Bathsheba, not to her. He should have realized that this would be a great sin against God, not just Bathsheba or her husband.

I believe the greatest protection we have from sin in these last days is a red-hot love for the Lord. Discipline and knowing the law are good things, but when it comes to the ultimate protection there is no match for love. Had David focused more on God's love for him rather than his lust for Bathsheba, he would have found himself in very different circumstances.

I am sure David regretted this decision the rest of his life, but he could not change it. The fear of the Lord could save you a lifetime of regret. Believe me, regret is a poor substitute for wisdom. If the devil is waving a temptation in front of your face that is so powerful you feel you are beginning to weaken, let me encourage you to look at the life of David. Look at the consequences he paid for his sin and I promise you the temptation you are facing will pale in the wake of its future destruction.

WEEK 25

REMEMBER LOT'S WIFE

Remember Lot's wife!
Luke 17:32

The second smallest verse in the New Testament stands as a classic lesson on the dangers of yearning for our old lifestyle after finding Jesus. It is not enough to get out of Egypt; Egypt must be taken out of us. Remember that Egypt in the Bible was always a type of the world. It is an amazing thing—when people pull away from God, they almost always go back to where they came from. If God delivered them from drugs, they go back to drugs. If God delivered them from alcohol, they go back to alcohol. Why? We always go back to that which we know and feel secure. Despite how rebellious some are, they still love security.

Change is a scary thing for most people and at best is only tolerated by the rest of us. Yet, it is only an absolute change of heart that can keep a person from going back to their old lifestyle. Behavior can be changed; geography can be changed; and even looks can be changed. However, if there is not a true change of heart, it is only a matter of time before the seductions of the things of the past come back and take up residence in the heart again.

Lot's wife had all the appearances of being saved. She was married to Lot, whom the Bible says was a righteous man. She was handpicked by God to be saved and taken out of Sodom and Gomorrah before He destroyed it. She hosted angels in her house, and they escorted her by hand out of her hellish environment. Her uncle was Abraham, the very father of our faith. Everything about her life seemed to be that of a godly woman. So why in the middle of His speaking on the second coming does Jesus tell us to remember Lot's wife? Because she, more than anyone else in the Bible, was a picture of a person who had every opportunity to be saved and had all the trappings of being saved, but never had a change of heart, a real relationship with God. She was surrounded by godly people who loved her, yet, she never made the decision to accept God for herself. She became so comfortable in her evil environment that, although God was able to take her out of the town, He could not change her heart which had grown to love and accept the evil all around her.

It is not enough to get out of Egypt; Egypt must be taken out of us.

Even after being warned by God not to look back, her affection for the things of her past won her over and God turned her into a pillar of salt. The things of this world can have a powerful pull on a person's heart. Lot's wife should serve as a reminder that we are to stay far away from the things of this world because even an angelic visitation may not be able to deliver us from their clutches!

WEEK 26

LOVE NEVER FAILS

**Love never fails. But where there are
prophecies, they will cease; where there
are tongues, they will be stilled; where
there is knowledge, it will pass away.**
I Corinthians 13:8

To say something never fails is a pretty bold statement.
In my life almost everything has failed at one time or
another. Sometimes my car does not start, my clothes wear
out, and even my faith wears pretty thin at times. I am really
glad there is one thing I can count on all the time—the love
of God. Even greater than His love is His unfailing love
toward me when I extend it toward others. Love shown to
others will always leave them in a better position than they
were before. Like matter, love cannot be destroyed. It may
take another form, but it is still love. Love can never be
wasted. You can never give too much love. Over a period of
time and in God's time, love will always bring about God's
desired result.

We will look at love in just a few of the many ways it
can be used. Probably one of the strongest characteristics
of love is its power to draw. Love is a magnet. A person who
has authentic love will attract the shy, the hurting, and the
hopeless. This is one of the reasons why crowds followed
Jesus wherever He went. Jesus loved people and people loved

Jesus. The hurting, the broken, the sick, and the lame—they all wanted to be around Him. Although He was not like them in that He walked in great authority and holiness, He loved them and wanted to help make them become more like Himself.

Like the rainbow, love has many colors. Love can draw a crowd and that same love can also disperse one. Just ask the money changers who were thrown out of the temple by Jesus. Love sometimes may look hard, even angry, but the test of love is always whose best interest it has in mind and what fruit it leaves behind. When Jesus cleared the temple, He was not trying to show how holy or powerful He was. He threw out the money changers to protect innocent people from other parts of the world, who in coming to worship God and make sacrifices to Him were being cheated by the money changers as they tried to turn their money into Jewish currency. Tough love is just as much love as nurturing or healing love.

Tough love is just as much love as nurturing or healing love.

Although its behavior can change, love always has the same pure motive. Sometimes parents must use tough love and stand between heaven and hell for their teenagers. That kind of love is no different than the love that nurtured and protected the teenager as a newborn child. Notice the methods are different but the motive is the same, which is to bring about good in the life of that child.

Another reason love never fails is that it has no specific time limit to bring about its desired result. Suffering cannot destroy love because love suffers long. Right now, you may be showing love to people and not seeing much in return.

Over time love will accomplish God's purpose. Love is patient and can wait out those people who are not in cooperation with it. Love will show kindness when treated unkindly. No matter what position you put love in, it will respond with desiring the best for all those involved. You cannot lose when you show love.

Keep in mind that you are not commanded to like everyone, but you are required to love them. To like someone means you share agreement in common values or interests. Love is a total different entity. We sometimes confuse the two but they are different as night and day. Two people with totally different backgrounds and lifestyles can love each other when fueled with the love of Christ.

Simply put, love never gives up. Just as the love of God has pursued us and has never given up on us, know that when shared with those around us, love will have the same effect. Perhaps you are struggling with someone you love who is not responding. Remember love never fails and it will bring about God's will and change—in His time. Be sure your motives are selfless and trust God for the rest.

WEEK 27

SHALL I HIDE FROM ABRAHAM?

When the men got up to leave, they looked down toward Sodom, and Abraham walked along with them to see them on their way.

Then the LORD said, "Shall I hide from Abraham what I am about to do?

Abraham will surely become a great and powerful nation, and all nations on earth will be blessed through him."

Genesis 18:16-18

From the beginning of time, man has always been obsessed with future events, especially those pertaining to himself. It was this tragic flaw in the life of Saul that eventually brought about his death. God, being our Creator, is well aware of this desire and for this reason, He has always given us ways to find out those things that were necessary for us to know. I want to add that there are times He chooses to teach us just to trust. Today, however, we want to look at God's desire to share vital information with those He loves.

In the Scripture above, we see the beginnings of a beautiful love relationship with God and Abraham, who is soon to be the father of many nations. We pick up on the story where God is about to destroy Sodom and Gomorrah because of the continual evil and sinful transgressions of the people in those two cities. He then brings up the thought-provoking question, **"Shall I hide from Abraham what I am about to do?" (verse17)** What God was really saying in that question is the topic of our writing. Was God saying He needed to inform Abraham of His actions, perhaps to get his permission? Not even close. What God was questioning was: Would it be wise to destroy these two cities, one of which Abraham's nephew, Lot, lived without first giving Abraham knowledge of what He was going to do? Here we see the tender consideration of God toward man. Did God need to inform Abraham? If He wanted to teach Abraham that He was a trustworthy God who would communicate honestly and openly with him—then yes, He did.

God is a revealer of secrets. He wants to involve man in the affairs of heaven. The problem is man is not always interested.

What God was doing was setting up the parameters for a lifelong relationship with the father of our faith. He was saying, "Abraham, you are so precious to Me that I will not do certain things without first informing you and at times even giving you a chance to question or intervene." It is important to see that God did not have to do this, but chose to do this to instill trust in Abraham. We see later in the chapter that God told Abraham of His plan, and allowed Abraham to intercede for the "twin cities," although to no avail. Is it not interesting that sometimes as Christians we think that just because we heard from God on an issue, we can do what we want and never inform those around us whose lives we affect? Even God shared information with those He loved before carrying out certain things that affected their lives.

It is important to see in this passage that God considers the lives of His servants before carrying out His will on earth. He talked with Noah before destroying the earth with water. He talked with Joseph before allowing the seven-year famine. Jesus warned His disciples of things to come before going to the cross. Psalm 25:14 tells us, **"The secret of the Lord is with them that fear him…"** (KJV). God is a revealer of secrets. He wants to involve man in the affairs of heaven. The problem is man is not always interested.

So let's think about it. You have your whole life ahead of you. You have many major decisions to make. Should I take this job? Should I marry this person? When should we begin to have children? The list can go on ad infinitum. Are we in this mess alone? Is the winner the one who makes the best guess? Not on your life!

Amos 3:7 tells us that **"Surely the Sovereign LORD does nothing without revealing his plan to his servants the prophets."** Be of good cheer! God has a plan for your future and He would love to begin to reveal it to you. You only need to believe that God cares about your life and begin to inquire of Him. God makes it clear that if we lack wisdom, we can call upon Him and get wisdom for every area of our lives (see James 1:5). God will be quick to hear your prayers and begin to guide you with His Spirit and truth.

WEEK 28

GOD'S GLASSES

**"For I know the plans I have for you," declares
the LORD, "plans to prosper you and not to harm
you, plans to give you hope and a future."
Jeremiah 29:11**

If God wore glasses and we could somehow borrow them
for a day, we would probably be quite surprised at what we
would see. They would probably make us look more powerful
than we really are, or perhaps they would make us look wise
and brave. And what about the ploys of Satan? Oh, they would
look obvious, even pathetic. Instead of these glasses being
called virtual reality glasses, they would be more like "are
you kidding me?" glasses because you would have a hard time
believing what you saw. You see, whenever God looks at us,
He does not see what we are, where we come from, or how
we are doing, but rather what He has created us to be. This
is why whenever He shows up on earth to talk to someone,
everyone has the same reaction, "Are you kidding me?" Let
us take a look at a few of these wonderful examples.

In Judges 6, we see that an angel of the Lord showed up
(this angel could have been God or maybe just an angel who
must have been wearing God's glasses). He greeted Gideon
by calling him a mighty man of valor. Gideon was a little
surprised by this greeting because he was hiding out from
the Midianites in a winepress, trying to bake a loaf of bread

to feed his family. To make matters worse, the angel had just called him a man of wealth and strength. Now it begins to get interesting. Gideon eventually realized that God had called him to destroy the very enemy he was hiding from, the Midianites. In fact, his very name meant warrior. For the first time Gideon began to see himself as God saw him. Until we begin to see ourselves as God sees us, we will live way beneath our privileges and not reach our destiny in Christ.

How about King David? Samuel ended up at the house of Jesse, his father, and was told by God to anoint one of Jesse's sons to be the next king of Israel. He looked over all of David's older brothers and could not seem to find a king. So, he asked Jesse just as a closing thought, "You don't happen to have any other sons hanging around, do you?" Sheepishly, Jesse answered that he had one more, but he was the youngest and he was out back tending sheep. Jesse was thinking that David was not king material. Jesse should have put his glasses on because

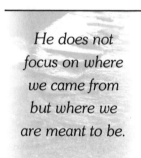

He does not focus on where we came from but where we are meant to be.

he was in for a big surprise. Soon after, David was anointed king (see I Samuel 16:3-12). You can bet there were a lot of "are you kidding me's?" going on at dinner that night. They probably were not wearing God's glasses either.

As you can see (no pun intended), God sees us much differently than we see ourselves. He looked at Mary, a virgin, and saw a mother. He looked at Abraham, the son of an idol maker, and saw the father of our faith. He looked at David, a shepherd boy, and saw a king. Perhaps a good term for this would be prophetic vision. Seeing what was meant to be, not what is.

So if God were to look at you, what would He see? More importantly, would you be seeing the same thing that He is seeing? The next time you are ready to rip into your children, how about asking God to borrow His glasses and then take a good look. Instead of reminding them of their failures, remind them of their destiny. This would actually be a good exercise in seeing and believing the best about all people. Praise God that He does not focus on our failures but rather our destiny. He does not focus on where we came from but where we are meant to be. You say, "Are you kidding me?" God says, "Why not?"

WEEK 29

ISOLATED MOMENTS

**The LORD had said to Abram, "Leave
your country, your people and your father's
household and go to the land I will show you.**

**I will make you into a great nation
and I will bless you; I will make your
name great, and you will be a blessing.**

**I will bless those who bless you, and whoever
curses you I will curse; and all peoples on earth
will be blessed through you."**

Genesis 12:1-3

Leave everything and everyone you know and start all over. I do not know about you, but to me those are some pretty serious commands. Yet, these are the Words of God to the father of our faith, Abraham, as he began his journey of knowing God. This was also the beginning of Abraham's schooling. God did not think it unreasonable to ask Abraham to leave everything behind and start a new life because He could supply everything Abraham needed for a new life. Actually things have not changed much since then. He still asks people to step out in faith, leaving all behind, so He can make something of them. So why did Abraham have to leave to begin again? Why couldn't he stay and accomplish the same thing?

In this writing we want to look at this Scripture from God's point of view. First of all, it is not so much that God needs a *new location* to work on us, but *we need isolation* to be worked on. Just as a surgeon needs an operating room free of all germs and hindrances when doing surgery, God needs isolation to perform spiritual surgery on us, to bring us to the new levels He desires for our lives. When it comes to making us into men and women of God, isolation is a requirement. Old friends and old places can sometimes be dangerous to the process of change.

Isolation teaches us to depend on God and God alone. Many times, when we are put into situations where we are being forced to grow or mature, our most normal reaction is to reach out to someone we know and see what they think. When in isolation, God is teaching us to go to Him and Him alone. For instance, Abraham was the son of an idol maker. What kind of godly advice do you think he would receive from his father in his quest to become a man of God? When God puts us in difficult situations, the first one He wants us to run to is Him. If necessary, He will tell us who to run to from there. God put Moses in isolation forty years in the desert, tending sheep. Joseph spent many years away from his family and homeland in Egypt being trained to one day lead that country and save the world. Before going to the cross, Jesus spent one long night alone in the Garden of Gethsemane. He wanted company, but God kept putting them to sleep. They could not be His security, only God could. These lonely times of isolation turned out to be the most fruitful times in each one of their lives. The fruit of isolation is meant to be intimacy. Obedience is required.

Isolation is schooling for exaltation in God.

Isolation can be a very lonely and discouraging thing. Sometimes during isolation, we think God has forgotten us and no longer plans to use us. As we learned in an earlier writing, waiting can be a dangerous time. In actuality, these isolated times are designed to make us more valuable in our work for God. It was during his time alone with God that Moses developed a relationship with God and learned that He could be trusted. It is a wonderful thing to be forced into the hand of God. It is by His divine design that these times are orchestrated in our lives.

You may be feeling like God has forgotten you and put you on the shelf. You may feel as if the promises He made to you no longer exist. Be of good cheer! Isolation is schooling for exaltation in God. God can only use men and women tried in the school of isolation. It is there where He molds and makes us fit for His purposes. It is during this time when we are meant to develop an intimate relationship with Him. Soon after graduation the crush of ministry will make that a much more difficult task!

WEEK 30

FAVOR'S PURPOSE

**And I will make of thee a great nation,
and I will bless thee, and make thy name
great; and thou shalt be a blessing.**

Genesis 12:2 (KJV)

God is a God of order. He does nothing without a divine purpose. All of His gifts are given to man to meet a need that man has. So it follows that those to whom God bestows favor, first and foremost, have a call by God to do a job that in the natural they are unable to do. Moses, a shepherd, needed to lead people, and Joseph, a young boy from a dysfunctional family, needed to lead a nation. Ruth, a widow who remained faithful to her mother-in-law, Naomi, had a need—to survive. So perhaps it is fair to say that one of the first requirements for obtaining favor is admitting we have a need. We cannot accomplish God's work without God's favor. In fact, we cannot lead a fruitful life without God's favor.

As a young pastor planting churches, I always found myself in a position of great need. I needed favor from almost everyone in the community, which is just what I found. From a landlord who gave us buildings to use for free, an employer who gave me a job for which I was not qualified, a banker who gave the church its first mortgage, and neighbors who chose to allow a church to be zoned in their neighborhood, favor was always in abundance. Without favor the job would never have been accomplished. This is why God never gives us jobs we can do without Him. If He did, we would be running off ahead of Him thinking that we could get the job done without Him. Unfortunately, we might get the job done but lose sight of His eternal purpose.

Noah was not a shipbuilder; he needed God. Moses was a murderer; he needed God. Joseph was not a skilled leader; he needed God. If you are doing something for God and you can do it without Him, beware—you will. God's favor is necessary for God's work. When God calls you to do a work for Him, He already has knowledge of where you will need favor. In actuality, favor waits on the obedient to show up at the right place and the right time. God prepared the brook at Kerith for Elijah well before he was in need of it (see I Kings 17:1-7).

We cannot accomplish God's work without God's favor.

Favor's purpose is simply to advance the kingdom and bring about God's will. To do this in a fallen world takes favor. It is the most exciting thing to see God bend the rules (so to speak) and push you to the place where He wants you to be because you are the servant He is using to do His bidding. Many times we do not even realize how favored we are until we are long into the project on which He has us working. While Joseph was in prison he probably did not think he was walking in the favor of God, but he was being prepared to save the world from famine. While Noah had been building the ark for one hundred years (it took one hundred twenty years to finish the project), he probably had thoughts like,

"What am I doing here?" But, it was through him and his family that the whole world started over again.

Favor has an incubation time, a time of preparation. In our world it is sometimes hard to recognize the favor of God. Remember God is not on our time schedule. His ways are not our ways (see Isaiah 55:8). Perhaps the greatest sign of God's favor is to walk in the fruit of His Spirit. To be able to walk in peace when the rest of the world is walking in fear and confusion is priceless. You may be asking yourself, "How do I fit into God's plan? Can I walk in favor?" Every life has a purpose and every purpose has needs. God's favor is for everyone. The choice is up to you, my friend. Seek God for your purpose and ask Him for His strength, wisdom, and favor to accomplish it. Remember, it is only when we seek favor's purpose that we receive favor's reward.

WEEK 31

GOD'S MADMAN

**At this point Festus interrupted Paul's defense.
"You are out of your mind, Paul!" he shouted.
"Your great learning is driving you insane."**
Acts 26:24

Paul was not mediocre about too many things in his life.
When he was a sinner, he did it with flair and passion.
Paul did not just talk bad about Christians; he did his part
to make them an endangered species. When it came to his
religion, he was equally committed. By his own words he was
a Pharisee of Pharisees (see Acts 23:6). Whatever Paul did,
he did it with excellence. The good news is, when he came
to know Jesus, he carried that same fire into his conversion.
After his conversion there was never any looking back. If
ever there was a man who believed Jesus Christ was Lord, it
was Paul. No matter where Paul was, he was found doing the
same thing—standing between heaven and hell battling for
the souls of men. It is no wonder that some people thought
he was a madman.

When Paul was going on trial for his life, we see him
more concerned for the lives of those who were putting him
on trial than his own life. Paul's attitude truly was for him to
live for Christ and to die was gain (see Philippians 1:21).
Although he lived in the world, his spirit was in constant
communication with his Lord. Was he a madman? Probably

not. Was he a man who was sold out? Most definitely. Is it not interesting that when Paul was sold out to the enemy and was killing Christians no one had much to say? Even the Christians he killed counted it an honor to be martyred for the cause of Christ. His persecution began when he changed teams and began turning his energies toward promoting the name of Jesus, the same name he previously was trying to destroy.

Not much has changed in the last two thousand years. The world we live in is still more comfortable with evil than good. High profile criminals and corporate greed are still looked at with a rather ho-hum attitude, while Christian men and women suffer much persecution for the cause of Christ. What was it about Paul that made him such a powerful witness for Jesus Christ even to the point of looking like a madman? First, we see Paul never minced his words. He spoke boldly about his God without apology as to how people would receive it. Whether it was a jailer or a governor, Paul spoke only one language—truth. I wonder how that would go over in the politically correct world in which we live? Paul also never seemed to mind the persecution that he received. Paul was not a complainer. In fact, he considered his persecution the proof of his ministry.

He refused to be polluted by the culture he was called to change.

Finally, Paul always put others before himself. His main concern was for the souls of those persecuting him. Even when he would rebuke some of leaders of the newly formed church, it was with their betterment in mind. In looking back, Paul did live like a madman. He refused to be polluted by the culture he was called to change. Despite how it was done before, Paul loved to work against the grain. He was every demon's nightmare—refer to the sons of Sceva (see Acts 19:13-16).

Perhaps the church today, as well as most of its preachers, could use a little bit of this madness. We have settled for being accepted by the world and instead have become infected by the world. May God grant us the grace and strength to stand up and be counted as peculiar. Sometimes "fitting in" is not a good fit at all.

WEEK 32

ATTITUDES THAT ATTRACT FAVOR

Then this Daniel was preferred above the presidents and princes, because an excellent spirit was in him; and the king thought to set him over the whole realm.

Daniel 6:3 (KJV)

Perhaps nothing can propel or hinder a person in their walk with God more than attitude. A person with a good attitude is one that God can work with easily and use to build His kingdom. A bad attitude first needs breaking down and changing before God can use it for kingdom business. As we look through the Bible and read about the many men and women who walked in great favor with God, we begin to see that they all had in common certain attitudes that helped invite the favor of God into their lives. In this writing we will look at some of the different attitudes that we will need to acquire as we begin to pursue God's favor. While I am sure that all these favored individuals possessed many godly attitudes that attracted His favor, we will try to isolate some of the main ones which separated these people from the rest of their peers.

The Bible says of Moses he was the meekest man on the earth (see Numbers 12:3). The word meek means "to have a proper attitude toward yourself, which means to know your strong and weak points and to **"not think of yourself more highly than you ought" (Romans 12:3)**. Meekness is controlled strength. In Moses' dealings with the Israelites, you see a godly humility that always put others first. God literally had to protect Moses even from his own brother, Aaron, and sister, Miriam, because he would not protect himself. Much like Jesus, who was also very meek and never defended Himself, Moses chose to let God do his fighting. However, Moses was not afraid to fight; he realized though if he protected himself, God would not. It should also be understood that a meek person is not a weak person. A meek person is a person who chooses

Satan will make the most noise right before your blessing is about to manifest.

to show mercy when he has every right and the authority to show strength or judgment. When Moses got angry with the Israelites for murmuring and complaining, he could have pronounced judgment for their sin, but instead he interceded for God to show mercy and not judgment.

The Bible says Daniel had **"an excellent spirit" (Daniel 6:3 KJV)**. Daniel excelled at everything he did. He was consistent and disciplined, and he did it all with an excellent spirit. Whether it was sticking to a diet or carrying out orders for his superiors, he always stood head and shoulders above those around him. So much so that the king placed him over all the princes and presidents of Babylon. As you could imagine, this did not sit well with everyone he was presiding over. So like many who get angry when they see the favor of God on another person's life, they began to make a plot against him. The only problem was that his life was so together and he walked in so much favor, they could not find anything against him. In Daniel 6:4 the Bible says, "...**he was faithful, neither was there any error or fault found in him**" (KJV). That is quite a nice little epitaph. Talk about a good report even from your enemies! Vince Lombardi would have loved him on his team. Bill Gates would have loved him on his board. Every wife would have loved him for a husband. They finally had to change the laws and make serving his God a crime. It did not take long before he was a criminal. Are you getting the point? Daniel served God with such fervency that nothing else mattered. He was quickly and easily convicted of being a godly man.

Another attitude necessary for attracting favor is faithfulness. We see this beautifully pictured in the life of Ruth. Whether it was being faithful to her mother-in-law, Naomi, and leaving all to follow after her, or following the requests of Boaz, Ruth was a faithful woman. This attitude, maybe more than any other is evident in the lives of all those who walked in great favor with God. Moses stayed faithful to God and the Israelites. Noah stayed faithful to God and the building of the ark. In very difficult circumstances, Joseph stayed faithful to God and the vision God had given him. Under even the most adverse circumstances, the faithful do not quit.

Many times people miss out on the blessings of God because they quit right before God is about to bless. Satan will make the most noise right before your blessing is about to manifest. Remember God's timing is perfect. Keep doing what He has sent you to do, and trust Him for the proper timing of your promotion and prosperity. Without faithfulness we will surely miss God's blessing, and with it we will be sure to receive His reward.

WEEK 33

CAN THESE DRY BONES LIVE?

**He asked me, "Son of man, can these bones live?"
I said, "O Sovereign LORD, you alone know."
Ezekiel 37:3**

Talk about a loaded question! Whenever God asks you a question there are always two things of which you can be sure: Number one, He knows the answer, and number two, He is pretty sure you either do not know the answer or do not want to give up the information. Take the first question ever recorded in God's Word. In Genesis 3:9, God asked Adam, **"Where art thou?"** (KJV) Fair enough question except for the fact that Adam knew he did not have a good answer. In this situation, I am pretty sure that it was the latter and not the former which was the case. Ezekiel, like most of us, was probably thinking this question was a little beyond his experience. Can dead bones live? Was this a challenge or was this a joke?

Since Ezekiel was a prophet, I am sure he was accustomed to many strange situations and instructions, but this was perhaps the strangest. In this passage we see God asked not only a difficult question, but then gave a difficult command— prophesy to these dead bones. How can we relate this passage to our lives today? What is God saying to us? Let us take a look and see how this passage speaks to our lives.

We are living in a fallen world with much pain and brokenness. Everywhere we look, we see sorrow written on the faces of people. Whether it is physical sickness, mental illness, poverty, divorce, or addiction, people's lives are filled with pain. Many live in situations where they seem helpless and there is no hope in sight. Hence, the big question: Can these dry bones live? Is there life after a devastating divorce? Can a child in bondage to drugs ever be normal again? Questions like these beg for an answer. More often than not, the world is silent. However, the church does not have to be. To these questions and many others like them, the answer is a resounding, "Yes!" These bones can live and it is God who provides the breath of life.

> *Whatever it is that you are going through today, speak the Word of the Lord to it.*

Perhaps you have been sinking in a situation that seems hopeless. You have prayed and sought God, seemingly without much success. Let me encourage you that with God all things are possible. He is only looking for those who will endure hardship like good soldiers so He can bring them the victory. Three simple keys to help bring back to life those things that we think are dead in our lives are: First we must be conscious that all things happen in His time. Faith must work with patience. God is not on our time schedule and we must wait in peace for His answers. In this microwave world we live in, we sometimes think if it does not happen fast, it is not going to happen. Remember, God sees the big picture and He does all things well. Do not let time rob you of your blessing.

Second, Romans 8:28 tells us that "...**God causes all things to work together for good to those who love God, to** those who are called according to His purpose" (NAS). It does not say all things are good but that they will work out for our benefit when we put God first in our lives. What a wonderful promise to hold onto in times of trouble. It is God that does the miracle, not you or me.

Finally, God told Ezekiel to prophesy the Word of the Lord to the bones and He would take care of the rest. Whatever it is that you are going through today, speak the Word of the Lord to it. Find the Scriptures that pertain to the situation that you are going through and speak to your mountain. Some mountains we are called to climb and some we are called to move. Either way God promises to bring you through. I pray that those dead things in your life will no longer speak of funerals, but a time of restoration and celebration.

WEEK 34

CONDITIONS

**For all the promises of God in him are yea,
and in him Amen, unto the glory of God by us.**

II Corinthians 1:20 (KJV)

I love the promises of God. In Christ, they are all ours, yea and amen! However, there is an interesting phenomenon about all of God's promises—in order to receive them, there is always a condition that must first be met. Much has been spoken about claiming His promises—little is said about walking out their conditions. You can go to most Christian bookstores and find numerous types of Bible promise books, but I have never seen a book of conditions. God wants us to trust Him and believe in His promises to us, but He also wants us to be able to walk out these conditions by faith.

Now at first it may seem that God put conditions before promises because He is trying to make it hard to obtain the promises. However, if you think about it carefully, instead of making it hard He could have never made the promises at all. The promises of God were His idea to bless us, not our idea to bless ourselves. So let us settle it in our minds that God put promises in His Word so that He had channels by which He could bless us. The conditions were also put there to bless us. You may be thinking: What are you talking about preacher? Let me explain.

Very often when we receive things easily, we do not put much value on them. An example of this is when missionaries in very poor countries charge a small amount for the pamphlets they would normally give out for free elsewhere. To the untrained eye this looks like they are being stingy and insensitive. However, the reason they do this is that when people with little money have to pay for the pamphlet, they value and take better care of it. Human nature tends to put more value on those things for which they pay a high price.

> *Meeting conditions is the price we pay for receiving God's promises.*

So in essence, meeting conditions is the price we pay for receiving God's promises. After we have put much effort and faith into receiving God's promises, we are less likely to let the devil come and steal them away without a fight. Many times, as the Scripture above notes, God has to patiently wait before He is able to give us what we need. Not because it takes Him a long time to get it to us, but because He does not want us to lose it as soon as we get it.

Another reason God puts conditions on His promises is to qualify who is serious about His kingdom. Careless answers invite more careless prayers. If God were to give blessings without cost, everyone would be in line. Remember, Jesus paid a great price in order for the blessings to be available to us. Now it is up to us to be obedient to God so He can turn this potential into reality.

The next time you think God is holding out on you to give you a hard time, remember the effort put into meeting the condition is building up your strength to hold onto the promise once it arrives. This is very much like the caterpillar who in its struggle to get out of the cocoon develops the strength to become a different creature that can fly. Likewise, when we meet the conditions of God's promises, we develop the strength to become new creatures in Christ, walking with new blessings we otherwise could never hold onto.

WEEK 35

NEEDS

**And without faith it is impossible to
please God, because anyone who comes
to him must believe that he exists and that
he rewards those who earnestly seek him.**

Hebrews 11:6

Some may be great and others small, but when it comes right down to it we all have needs. If God were moved by needs, India would be a nation in revival. If God were moved by needs, hospitals would be more on fire than most churches. If God were moved by needs, I would be a spiritual giant. Yet God is not moved by needs, but by faith.

Throughout the Bible, we plainly see that Jesus, although He had great compassion, often passed by the needy—but He was always moved by faith. Probably the highest compliment we can pay to a person is to simply trust him. So when we put our faith in God, it pleases Him more than anything else. If faith moves the heart of God, then doubt and unbelief must break it. Let us take a look at some of the people who moved the heart of God with their faith, so we may also become God movers and not heartbreakers.

In Matthew 8, the story of the centurion whose servant was sick unto death is one that clearly shows how God is moved by faith. First, we see he had enough faith to send his servants to seek after Jesus. His faith was an aggressive faith, not one that laid back and waited. His faith was moved by the urgency of his need. Second, we see that his faith was so strong that he did not need to see Jesus in person. Being a centurion he understood authority. He understood the power of the spoken word. He not only understood, but also believed that if Jesus would just speak the word, his servant would be healed. This was the very thing that shocked Jesus. Only two times in the Bible does it mention that Jesus marveled—the other time was at the lack of faith of certain people (see Mark 6:6). This time, however, He was moved by the powerful faith of this centurion. Simply put, when it comes to pleasing God nothing does it better than a red-hot faith in Him.

Another person who moved the heart of God with his faith was Abraham, the father of faith. In Romans 4 the Bible mentions a few of the characteristics that made Abraham one of the heroes of our faith. First, it says that against hope he believed in hope. Despite all the things that kept pointing to how impossible it was to receive what God had promised him, he kept his faith in God and God's ability to bring it to pass, not his (if you remember his interlude with Hagar, you realize he did not always have this quality). Also, Abraham was fully persuaded that God was able to do what He said He would do. Abraham had been in enough difficult situations to know that God was able to do His part.

If faith moves the heart of God, then doubt and unbelief must break it.

Today you may be thinking: Why is God not doing anything? Does He not see I have such great needs? Yes, God sees your needs, but He is looking for your faith. It is time to realize that if we are going to please God it can only be with our faith. Determine today to take your eyes off of your needs and focus them on the God who said He is able to meet them. Begin to praise Him and thank Him for the needs He has already met. It will not be long before He will be moving again in your life. The needs you thought you had will be opportunities for God to show His power and love toward you. Needs are everywhere. Dare to be a man or woman of faith and move the heart of God by your trust in Him.

WEEK 36

SAVED...BUT FROM WHAT?

How can a young man keep his way pure?
By living according to your word.
Psalm 119:9

You hear it all the time. You need to get saved. It is great to be saved. Jesus saves! But do people really understand what they need to get saved from? If you were to listen to most of the television and radio preaching on the air today, we need to be saved because we need help for all the troubles we have to deal with in this life. In other words, God sent Jesus to save us from our troubles. Now I do believe that in times of trouble our God is a God who will help deliver us. I do believe that when we call upon Him in these times He will be quick to come to our aid. However, we must realize that Jesus did not die on the cross to save us from our troubles, but to save us from our sins. Sin, by the way, is the cause of most of our troubles.

Despite all the Christian resources available in this country, this is one of the reasons the church today is stagnant and people are not coming to know the Lord like we hoped. If you are looking for a way out of your troubles, there are many sources available. Lawyers, doctors, counselors, and accountants all make a good living helping people get out of their troubles. Depressed? Go see a counselor. Falling into debt rapidly? See a credit counselor. On the other hand, if you are looking to break the power of sin in your life, there is only one answer. His name is Jesus.

The world will often help a person change their behavior or lifestyle. People fill rehabs and prisons; their behavior is forced to change but this type of change is fueled by the discipline and desire that an individual may have to change. The problem is, once they are put in front of the temptations that previously conquered them, more often than not they fall. Not because they did not have discipline or desire, but because true change did not take place in their heart.

The only way to truly change a person is to change their heart. This is why Jesus said **"...where your treasure is, there will your heart be also" (Matthew 6:21 KJV)**. If a person treasures alcohol, and he goes into rehab for a year which changes his environment and behavior, this will seem like the right idea. The problem is that if his heart has not been changed, as soon as he has his freedom back, very often his heart will seek after the same treasure that brought him pleasure.

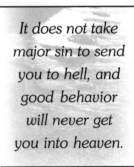

It does not take major sin to send you to hell, and good behavior will never get you into heaven.

So you see, to really understand what we have been saved from, we must understand how wicked our hearts are. The prophet Jeremiah tells us that our hearts are **"...desperately wicked: who can know it?" (Jeremiah 17:9 KJV)**. This is why Jesus warns us in Matthew 7 about judging another person. We may be surprised to know that the same evil which has manifested in another person may lie dormant in our heart, but the quickest way to wake it up is to cast our judgment on them.

Perhaps you may be thinking, "I'm not really that bad of a person. I do not have any major sins or vices in my life." This kind of thinking is dangerous for two reasons. First of all, it does not take major sin to send you to hell, and good behavior will never get you into heaven. We have all been born with a heart bent toward evil. As we get older, it comes more natural to move toward and act upon that evil. Second, only those who have been forgiven much love much. The more you realize how badly you need a Savior, the more you will love the Savior. Many people live marginal Christian lives because they do not realize the great gift that has been given to them. Begin today to make Christ your treasure and you will be pleasantly surprised to see how your heart will follow after Him. Then, and only then, will you know how good it feels to be saved and realize what you have been saved from.

WEEK 37

IDOL GIFTS OR IDLE GIFTS

The body is a unit, though it is made up of many parts; and though all its parts are many, they form one body. So it is with Christ.

and the parts that we think are less honorable we treat with special honor. And the parts that are unpresentable are treated with special modesty,

while our presentable parts need no special treatment. But God has combined the members of the body and has given greater honor to the parts that lacked it.

I Corinthians 12:12, 23-24

In the modern culture of today's church there seems to be two extremes—people are either not using their gifts or they are idolizing certain gifts and forgetting the whole purpose of the gifts is to serve one another. I have often heard in the body, "I can't do that; it's not my gift." Both of these situations are extremes and not healthy for the body of Christ. The church has made too big of a deal about certain popular gifts and have ignored many others. Let us look at these two extremes and see how we might bring them into balance.

The Bible makes it clear that we have all been given gifts and they are to be used to serve the body of Christ (see I Corinthians 12:7). Whether it is one of the nine spiritual gifts or the gift of encouragement, etc., all of our gifts are necessary in the body of Christ. There is no gift that is more necessary than another. Preaching is a wonderful gift. However, if everyone had that gift there would be no one left to listen, and therefore, the gift would be useless. The reality is that everyone has something to give to the body of Christ and we should be careful not to look for only those gifts that bring attention or notoriety.

Perhaps the main reason God gives each one of us a gift is so we have some way to serve and fit into the body of Christ.

Thank God for the carpenter who will fix the leaky church roof or the cleaning person who keeps the church building looking nice. You might be saying, "Well that is not a gift; anyone can do that." It is this type of thinking that causes people to try to be what they are not, which is one of the reasons why the church is so weak. By idolizing a few gifts and those people, we cause others to want the same attention and then they seek after those gifts. After all, why serve as an usher when I can be the preacher? People are struggling to find their place in the body of Christ and we are only recognizing a few positions.

The helps ministry, which used to be the backbone of the church, has dwindled in favor of everyone needing to go to school to become the pastor or teacher. Please understand, as a pastor I can appreciate if someone has the call of God on his or her life to pastor. In that case nothing else will satisfy. We must, however, be careful that we do not push people into ministry who should be staying behind to help those already called. I strongly believe that one of the reasons so many people are leaving the ministry is because they were never supposed to be there in the first place. They were sent in a direction by overzealous Christians who believed that the only way to serve God was to be a full-time minister. Because of this, many called pastors are laboring under extremely heavy loads while their help has been told the only way to serve is to go off to school and become a preacher.

Now on the other side of this coin are those sitting on their gifts not using them at all. It will probably come as no surprise that in church a small minority of the people do the great majority of the work. Eventually, that small group of people get worn out while those not using their gifts get bored and walk away from church thinking: Is that all there is?

Perhaps the main reason God gives each one of us a gift is so we have some way to serve and fit into the body of Christ. When we do not use our gifts we get lost in the outskirts of church life—sometimes for good. One of the lies the devil has us believing is that if we do not use our gift, we will lose our gift. That is simply not true.

The Bible teaches us that "...**the gifts and calling of God are without repentance**" (**Romans 11:29** KJV). The truth is that when a person does not use their gift, the body loses. The body loses out on one of the parts meant to be a blessing; it also usually means, some of the other parts will have to work that much harder.

So are you sitting on one end of these extremes? Are you not using your gift, or perhaps, wanting to use only the gift you were given and not serving where needed? I am a preacher, but I have cleaned toilets and changed light bulbs. I have found that the most important gift in the church is the one needed at the moment. Let me encourage you today to find the gift that God has given to you and use it to be a blessing to the body of Christ. This is when you will begin to know the excitement of walking in your gift and realize your value to the body of Christ.

WEEK 38

WORKING IN THE DARK

**Now faith is being sure of what we hope for
and certain of what we do not see.
Hebrews 11:1**

No one exemplified working in the dark more than Noah. By this I mean Noah walked in obedience with no visible sign of the fruit for his labor. He had never built an ark nor had he seen rain, yet, he was obedient to God's command for one hundred twenty years. He began with his family and when it was time to close the hatch, that is who he ended with. The Bible says he was a preacher of righteousness, and yet one hundred twenty years later not one person was changed by his life or ministry. There are many other people who have worked in the dark—Moses, Joseph, and Daniel to name a few. They all did a lot of work in the dark, but no one labored longer and seemingly had less fruit to show for his labor than Noah.

So what can we learn from this man who worked tirelessly and faithfully for this long period of time with seemingly little fruit to show for it? Let me start by saying Noah ended up with a tremendous amount of fruit—from his family the entire world was repopulated after the flood. Indirectly, you and I and all the inhabitants of the earth are a result of

Noah's faithfulness. All of a sudden we now realize that Noah had a tremendous amount of fruit. He just did not get to see much of it. Hence, we have the title "Working in the Dark." Here are a few words of encouragement to those working in the dark who are not seeing too many prayers answered or great works being done.

The first thing we see about people who work in the dark is that they all heard God clearly in the light and never doubted Him in the dark. God is not a man that He should lie (see Numbers 23:19). What He has promised He will bring to pass if we remain faithful to our calling. These men never looked to the world around them for affirmation. They received all of their encouragement from their heavenly Father. If you look around and judge your life by how those around you respond, you will be sorely disap-

> *If you are going to struggle, it should be to hear God right the first time.*

pointed. Get your marching orders directly from God. This also means that you should not become too elated if things are going really well. The same crowd that shouted, "Hosanna glory to God in the highest" (see Matthew 21:9) when Jesus was coming into town on a colt, crucified Him one week later. People change their minds like the wind changes its direction. Only God remains faithful to His Word and the calling on your life. If you are going to struggle, it should be to hear God right the first time. Once you have heard Him, never look back.

Jesus is the light in your darkness. Never allow people or situations to substitute for the light of God in our lives. When God calls a person to accomplish something, He will provide the finances, the giftings, and the favor necessary to get the job done. He is responsible to be your Provider. I might add however, God almost always uses others around us to bring us to these different levels. He has done this for me many times in my life. Be careful to recognize those whom God has brought into your life and discern whether or not they may be a gift from God.

Another way of saying "working in the dark" could be "walking in faith." You see faith will bring you into some pretty dark places. Praise God for the light of Jesus that can light up even the darkest situations. If you feel like you have been working for God with seemingly no visible results, remember many of God's greatest servants did not get to see their results. However, their work stood the test of time and influenced many generations beyond their own. Perhaps the greatest compliment God can pay any of us is to have our works outlast our lives. This is the true success that we should always be seeking. So for now—keep your flashlights on.

WEEK 39

THE DIRTY THIRTY

**Then one of the Twelve—the one called
Judas Iscariot—went to the chief priests
and asked, "What are you willing to
give me if I hand him over to you?"
So they counted out for him thirty silver coins.
Matthew 26:14-15**

Thirty pieces—that is all it took to buy Judas' help in betraying Jesus. That is all it took for Judas to forget all the miracles, the fellowship, and love that Jesus had shown him. To his credit, he eventually did realize his blunder and even tried to give back the money, but it was too late. Satan had already convinced Judas that he was no good and had no reason left to live. Shortly after this, Judas took his own life. How sad that after all the time Judas spent with Jesus, he did not realize there was forgiveness even for this horrible sin. That Jesus died for all of our sins is a biblical fact. An amazing thing that I have noticed after twenty-five years of ministry is that people often do not feel they are worthy to be forgiven.

If we are really honest, we all have a price and Satan knows what it is. Your price may be power, money, another woman or man, but we all have an Achilles' heel. If we do not walk diligently, Satan will be able to reach us with his goods. The truth is, every day we have chances to sell out to the enemy and to give in to the weakness and flaws of our flesh. Every day we must choose to say no to the "dirty thirty" that comes our way. You would think that after a while we would notice the enemy when he encroaches on our ground, but I submit that most of the time he comes by our invitation.

Judas did not get greedy overnight. It was probably a lifelong struggle that he never dealt with. I think there is a good chance that Jesus knew he had the problem but still made him treasurer of the ministry. Jesus probably allowed it so that under His careful watch, Judas would finally deal with it. However, that did not happen. What could have been an easy fix turned out to be the final word on his life: Here lies a man who refused to deal with his sin. Samson had the same problem, just a different outlet. He also did not come to lust overnight (see Judges 14:3). It was something he probably dealt with for years before he met Delilah. Just like Judas however, when the final exam came, he flunked miserably.

It is a lot easier to put out a spark than a raging fire.

So now that we realize we all have weaknesses and we all have a price, we will all be prepared when the enemy comes— right? Here are a few quick tips to help pull the "FOR SALE" sign off the front lawn of our hearts. The Bible tells us if **"...we would judge ourselves, we should not be judged" (I Corinthians 11:31 KJV)**. As we mentioned earlier about Judas and Samson, their character flaws did not become fatal overnight. It is a lot easier to put out a spark than a raging fire.

Deal with sin quickly before it takes control of your life. Enlist God's help in winning the battle. He alone can give you the victory. Whatever it is you are struggling with, declare it your enemy. God promises to deliver us from our enemies, not our friends. Finally, find a pastor or trusted leader you can share your burden with and have them hold you accountable in that area. Accountability is vital in winning the war over a sin problem.

It is very easy to sit back and think of Judas as a moral and human failure, but truthfully any weakness left unchecked in our lives has the ability to grow like a cancer—out of control which can lead us to total destruction. When we are humble and realize we have a weakness, God will always give us strength to overcome any adversity when we cry out to Him for help.

WEEK 40

HOW AM I DOING?

But the Lord said to Samuel, "Do not look at his appearance or at the height of his stature, because I have rejected him; for God sees not as man sees, for man looks at the outward appearance, but the Lord looks at the heart."
I Samuel 16:7 (NAS)

During the time I was growing up in New York, we had a colorful mayor by the name of Ed Koch. Mayor Koch's claim to fame was always asking others, "How am I doing?" In order to keep his hand on the pulse of the people of New York, he would constantly solicit their input. This is a great idea for a politician who lives or dies by the votes of the people. However, when it comes to serving God, this can lead to spiritual suicide. When it comes to how we are doing on our journey with the Lord, there are a few things that are vital to our success in serving God and reaching our destiny in Him.

Man looks for different things in leadership than God. There is a major difference between being voted in by man and being called by God. It can be very dangerous as well as disheartening to look to people to encourage you to do a job that only God called you to do. Very often people will not even recognize the call of God on your life when you first begin. When Israel began to look for an earthly king (much to God's displeasure), it was the first time God allowed them to choose. Their choice was Saul. They chose him primarily because he looked good on the outside—which is pretty much the only thing man sees. He was a strong warrior, handsome, and had a lot of charisma. These may seem to be qualities of a leader, but they are dangerous if they belong to a man who is not called by God or to a man who loses his desire to please God along the way.

When Israel looked for a king the second time, God chose David mainly because he possessed a heart that pleased God and pursued Him. It was a surprise to everyone, but God saw his heart. God knew everything else could be developed over a period of time as David walked with the Lord.

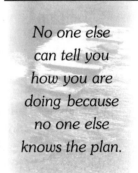

No one else can tell you how you are doing because no one else knows the plan.

The Bible teaches us that **"the fear of man brings a snare..." (Proverbs 29:25 NAS)**. The fear of man is a trap. We must always be more concerned about what God may think about a situation than man. Churches are dying all over the country because the leadership has been more concerned about getting people in the seats rather than God in the pulpit. They put more effort into having people show up at the services than they do the presence of the Holy Spirit. I am sure most of these people are God-fearing people who love God deeply. They have just bought into the notion that if the church is full there is a better chance that God will show up. This is not necessarily true. Very often in the Bible you will see that God reduces before He produces.

Moses was a wonderful example of a godly leader. Although he started out a little shaky, when it came to getting directions, encouragement, or even correction, Moses never looked horizontally but always vertically. Moses knew that the secret to kingdom leadership was to get your information directly from the King. If he were to look at the hearts and attitudes of the people, he would have certainly been discouraged and turned back.

Daniel was another beautiful example of this principle. Not only did he never look to his earthly peers for confirmation or direction, but he was so obviously heavenly-minded that they had to change the laws of the nation to catch him in his only predictable position—praying to his God on a regular basis.

"How am I doing?" It works great in politics because the people who called you into office are the only ones who can keep you there. So in essence, if you are going to be a politician voted in by the voice and vote of the people, it might be wise to hear what they think. However, you must remember that if you are called of God to carry out His destiny for your life, He alone knows the plan. No one else can tell you how you are doing because no one else knows the plan or whether or not you are sticking to it. I am not saying that we should not encourage each other; it is certainly biblical to do so. However, we should also encourage each other to go to God for our encouragement and direction. Our encouragement should matter little unless it is to tell that person to continue to be faithful in seeking out the will of God in his life.

One of the most important things we can do today is realize Who called us. Only then will we not waver at the words of people. When Aaron listened to what the people wanted, it caused him much grief. Develop an ear and a desire to know God's voice; it will save you much grief and bring you much joy on your journey.

WEEK 41

MORAL AMNESIA

**Therefore if anyone is in Christ, he is a
new creature; the old things passed away;
behold, new things have come.
II Corinthians 5:17 (NAS)**

Amnesia is defined as "a loss of memory." Sometimes after a traumatic blow to the head, a person may forget a major part of his past life. I like to think of moral amnesia as what happens when a person comes out of the world and gets wonderfully and radically saved, but forgets the muck and mire from which God delivered him. At first, forgetting the past may sound like a wonderful thing—even a scriptural thing—however, it becomes dangerous when people only forget *their own* pasts. They know they have been cleansed by the blood of Jesus and forgiven of all past sins. They are now new creatures in Christ. The problem occurs when they are looking at others' sins and failures and they forget the mercy and grace that God showed them, becoming judgmental and harsh toward those struggling to get free.

If you were to ask those with moral amnesia about their lives before Christ, they would be able to clearly tell you all the deep, dark details of their lives without God and how He wonderfully and gloriously saved them. However, when they look at the lives of those around them, rather than look through the filter of love and grace, they take this attitude: If God did this for me, why did He not do this for you?

A person with moral amnesia will talk about the pig trough that God delivered them from, but will have very little tolerance for the person who is still stuck in the pig trough. This is exactly the opposite of the way it should be. The fact that we are trophies of a certain lifestyle should also be our calling card to help us reach that lifestyle. The Bible clearly teaches that the person whom has been forgiven much should also love much (see Luke 7:47).

I am convinced that the cause of moral amnesia also has to do with something that happened to our heads. However, it is not a blow to our heads but the swelling of it. When we begin to think the reason we are free is because of something we did or something we are, we are in danger of needing another blow to our heads—this time from God. If Satan cannot kill you with your favorite sin, he will try to kill you with pride which tells you that you had something to do with your own deliverance. It is by God's mercy and grace that we are both saved and delivered. He alone gives us the strength to get free and stay free. We should take very little credit for any of our victories, but give all the glory to God.

> We should take very little credit for any of our victories, but give all the glory to God.

One of the places moral amnesia strikes most often is with parents disciplining their children. Some parents who are saved at thirty and get their lives together for the first time will often be very harsh on their wayward child, forgetting the patience and love God showed toward them and the time it took for His love to sink in and make a change in their lives. Much damage can be done to our children when we judge them from our newly elevated place in Christ, rather than loving them and remembering the snares of the world and how easy it was to get trapped. Jesus, who was sinless and perfect in all ways, treated the woman at the well with love and mercy knowing the weaknesses of the flesh. The religious leaders, however, were quick to rush to judgment. They did not want to deal in grace, but rather the letter of the Law. Jesus, who knew no sin, knew how to deal with it better than those who were quite competent at it (see John 4:1-42).

Remember, it is by grace that we are saved, not by our works. You may be living a new life in Christ, but remember all of our righteousness is still as filthy rags compared to the holiness of God (see Isaiah 64:6). Use patience and grace when dealing with your lost loved ones. Do not be too quick to forget the pain of your past bondage and let it be a gentle persuader to help set others free. *Forget your sins, but remember His grace.* Only by doing this will you be able to use your past to give others a future.

WEEK 42

STAY ON THE WHEEL

This is the word that came to Jeremiah from the LORD:

"Go down to the potter's house, and there I will give you my message."

So I went down to the potter's house, and I saw him working at the wheel.

But the pot he was shaping from the clay was marred in his hands; so the potter formed it into another pot, shaping it as seemed best to him.

Jeremiah 18:1-4

Almost twenty-five years ago, when I was a young man in Bible school, one of the great missionaries of our denomination came to speak at our chapel service. His name was Charles Greenaway and his message was, "Stay on the Wheel." I do not really remember much of the message, but the title never left me. I believe the main point of his message was this: When things get tough, do not quit; do not give up; and do not jump off the Potter's wheel. That being said, I want to take some time to look at the benefits of staying on the wheel. Many times we miss out on the blessings of God in our lives because we get off the Potter's wheel before God is finished working on us. One thing I have learned in my thirty-five years of serving God is that whenever we miss a test of character or faith, there will always be another chance to retake it. Yes, God always gives make-up exams, and we do not get promoted until you pass.

People get off the wheel for a myriad of reasons, but it will not keep them from making up their "wheel time." God is pretty serious about wheel time. You see, wheel time is really preparation time to enable us to accomplish our mission. He allowed Moses forty years of tending sheep to prepare him for forty years of leading people. I wonder which was harder? Jesus spent thirty years for a mere three years of ministry. Paul spent close to three years in the desert to prepare for a grueling ministry of preaching the gospel like a madman while enduring the same persecution he had given Christians.

God always gives make-up exams, and you do not get promoted until you pass.

Now let us get back to a few reasons why people get off the wheel. Some people get off the wheel because they get tired of the pain. When God is molding and shaping our lives, it is the equivalent of spiritual surgery. It can be painful to see ourselves as we really are, but even more painful to have to try to make changes. Much of our suffering is God exposing our sin to us so we can deal with it and move on. The key is, not moving on until we deal with what God has revealed.

Many people get off the wheel because the wheel is a lonely place. Part of God making and molding us into His image is getting our eyes off of everything and everyone else so that we focus only on Him. That usually translates to loneliness. Perhaps aloneness might be a better word since one of the purposes of wheel time is to be alone with God and get to intimately know Him.

Still another reason people jump off the wheel is they see everyone else doing it and seemingly staying alive. It is not that we cannot live off the wheel; God, in fact, gives us the free will to jump off. If, however, we want to accomplish God's will for our lives and live life more abundantly, we will eventually have to get back on the wheel and allow Him to finish the process.

These are just a few of the many reasons why people get off the Potter's wheel and stop God from completing His work in them. Because we have free will, God will always allow us to jump on and off the wheel at our desire, but remember we do not get to skip any of the process. Jonah robbed that great fish of a good meal when he decided to get back on the wheel. Thankfully, God will always allow us to be obedient when we decide we are ready. One little side note: We can do a lot of damage trying to get ready—damage which will have both fleshly as well as eternal consequences. Quite honestly it is easier to stay on the wheel.

Maybe you have jumped off the wheel and are not sure how to get back on. The quickest and easiest way to get back on the wheel is to go back to where you were disobedient and make it right with God. Jonah got back on the wheel, but he still had to go to Ninevah. He did not get to choose a new mission. Every obedience to God prepares you for the next challenge. Therefore, being obedient each day is important to meet the challenge of the next. Perhaps the greatest challenge of the wheel is learning to trust God with your life. When you allow God to have His will in your life and you accept it no questions asked, the wheel begins to slow down and you may then get your chance to walk off—with God's blessing.

WEEK 43

LOCATION!
LOCATION!
LOCATION!

**"Bless the LORD, all his works in all places of
his dominion: bless the LORD, O my soul."**

Psalm 103:22 (KJV)

They call it the three L's of real estate. When it comes to
value in real estate, the only thing that really matters
is location. In some ways it is not much different in the
spiritual realm. God often has to put people in certain places
to get the most out of them. As humans, we sometimes get
too comfortable in the same place after a while. Equally
important, however, is for God to bless a *place* when He has
put one of His chosen in that place. That's right, we can
bring blessing wherever we go.

Many times we find ourselves in locations that do not
look very desirable. God's addresses, you see, are often in
troubled neighborhoods. I think it has something to do with
being lights in dark places. More than once I have questioned
God as to why I was in a certain area or situation and I always
receive the same answer: He will choose the place and I must
choose obedience.

The great apostle Paul found himself in some pretty hard places. He was not usually given the key to the city for most of the places he went. In fact, he was usually run out on a rail or left for dead. Paul was perhaps the greatest of all the New Testament characters, but still did not get too many good locations. He never had a church that really loved or took good care of him. He never even had a Pastor Appreciation Dinner, but that never stopped him. He was a preaching machine whose attitude was, "**...to live is Christ, and to die is gain" (Philippians 1:21 KJV).**

Jonah also had some pretty bad locations. He was told to go preach in Nineveh, the cruel enemy of his people—he chose the high seas. He ended up in one of the most unique locations ever noted in the Bible, the belly of a great fish. He finally agreed to go to Nineveh and the whole nation got saved (see Jonah 3). Moses was sent to the Promised Land but spent all his time circling in the desert trying to get in. Joseph was sent to Egypt and Daniel to Babylon; neither were very savory locations for Hebrew children of the Most High God.

God's addresses, you see, are often in troubled neighborhoods.

Are you beginning to see the two-fold reason of bad locations? Jesus put it this way: "**...They that be whole need not a physician, but they that are sick" (Matthew 9:12 KJV).** In other words, if you want to catch fish, you have to go where the fish are. If you are going to be a light, your only use can be in darkness. If you have good news, it must be preached to those who are bad news. Wherever God sent His servants, He matured them, provided for them, and blessed the people to which He sent them. Daniel became a great leader in Babylon. Joseph saved not only Egypt, but also the whole world from famine, and Jonah kept Nineveh from being destroyed by God. Not bad work for some pretty bad locations.

Maybe you are reading this thinking: Why has God left me in this godless town or city? Perhaps you are in a loveless marriage or a dysfunctional family—you can be the lifeline that brings hope and salvation to those you love. You may be a pastor who feels that his location is just not suitable to grow a church. Remember, God put some of His choicest servants in some of the most difficult locations. Never judge your worth by your location. Jesus did His *greatest work* in pretty bad locations.

WEEK 44

THE FRUIT
OF FAVOR

**"If you are pleased with me, teach me your ways
so I may know you and continue to find favor with
you. Remember that this nation is your people."**

**The LORD replied, "My Presence will go
with you, and I will give you rest."**

Exodus 33:13-14

As we have previously discussed, the favor of God is something that we find, or perhaps, it finds us. Either way, once God's favor is on your life, you will never be the same. I want to make it clear that although favor has many fruits, today we are going to be looking at the fruit of God's presence. In this passage, we see Moses questioning God as to whether or not he had indeed found God's favor in his life. This was probably a wise thing to do as Moses had the lives of well over one million Jews in his hands. His decisions were vital to the welfare of these people. He had very little margin for error and much to lose if he was mistaken. It is interesting to see what Moses asked for as proof of God's favor.

First, let us see what he did not ask for. He did not ask for an easier life or some type of vindication toward those that were giving him a hard time—although there were many. He also did not ask for outward signs of prosperity or material gain, although prosperity is often a sign of God's favor. What he did ask for, however, was that he would know and understand God's ways. This is very much like Solomon's request for wisdom to lead God's people. These were godly men in serious situations. They were not looking for their own lives to be benefited, but rather the lives of those for whom they were responsible. Keep in mind by making these wise choices that their lives benefited greatly. You will never hurt yourself when, in obedience to God, you are reaching out to help others.

When it comes right down to it, favor is knowing God— period. Favor is knowing that God has heard your prayer and has full intentions of answering it. Favor is knowing God's thoughts on a situation. It is knowing what God's plans are at a particular time and how He wants them carried out. Favor is not the ability to see problems; life is filled with critics and people with the ability to see problems. Favor is having answers to those problems and bringing God's presence and grace into a situation.

Favor is not only for your life, but the lives of those around you.

God told Joseph that there was going to be a worldwide famine for seven years and that he could avert tragedy by saving food for the seven years before the famine. Such intimate knowledge of future events and wisdom on how to deal with them can only come from God. Because Joseph was obedient, civilization as we know it was spared and Joseph's favor became everyone's blessing. Favor is not only for your life, but the lives of those around you. Noah's favor saved humanity from being totally destroyed by water. Ruth's favor saved the life of her mother-in-law, Naomi. As you can see, God uses favor in the lives of those He can trust to bless and bring salvation to those who otherwise might perish.

After seeing what a valuable and wonderful thing it is to have the favor of God in your life, it is no wonder that everyone would want it. Now the question is: Are you willing to pay the price of obedience to God and are you willing to use your favor to help others as He directs? God's favor is given to those He can trust. Today, make it your desire to be one of God's trusted servants and ask Him not just to bless you but make you a blessing. You will see that in seeking the benefit of others, you will be equally blessed.

WEEK 45

SABBATH OR DAY OFF

Remember the sabbath day, to keep it holy.
Exodus 20:8 (KJV)

Hidden among the "Thou Shalt Nots" of the Ten Commandments is this no less important yet equally demanding commandment. Here in the United States, days off are synonymous with going to the doctor, getting a hair cut, mowing the lawn, or other things we consider leisure activities. For years, I broke this commandment fearlessly. I thank God for His mercy, but I often wonder how much more fruitful I would have been had I taken this commandment more seriously.

The word "Sabbath" literally means "to cease, to make to rest." It does not mean to do work we do not get paid for like most of us do on our days off. God was so serious about rest that on the seventh day of creation, He chose to model this very important part of our life. I find it very interesting that eight of the Ten Commandments began with **"thou shalt not,"** but when it came to the Sabbath, God said **"remember."** We are unique creatures. We have to be *commanded* not to do evil and *reminded* to do something good.

You will also notice that along with rest, God reminded us to keep the Sabbath holy. So, the Sabbath was not just a ceasing of activities, but a time to draw close to God and reflect on His goodness and mercy in our lives. I believe this had to be a commandment for that reason. It would be the greatest thing in the world to be commanded not to go to work. It is quite another story to tell someone they can stay home but they need to rest and refresh their walk with God. Add to this the Protestant work ethic—you do not get anything for nothing—and you begin to understand why we live in a society of overworked and exhausted people. Many of those are Christians, who feel guilty when they take time to rest and reflect.

Like almost everything in the Old Testament, God was very exacting about the Sabbath. On that day you could not work, and you could not collect food. Luckily eating was left optional. The Pharisees were such sticklers about this law that they even got upset when Jesus healed a man on the Sabbath (I guess going to the doctor would have been out of the question). Here is the key to understanding the Sabbath in our New Testament way of thinking. As usual, it took Jesus to put into perspective all the confusion surrounding this very unique day. Simply put, He said "**...The Sabbath was made for man, not man for the Sabbath**" (**Mark 2:27**). In other words, the Sabbath was made to benefit and be a blessing to us. We need the Sabbath; the Sabbath does not need us. Thank you, Jesus, for reminding us.

Make it your focus to take this very special time each week to get alone with God and rest your body from the never-ending stress of living in a fallen world. The way to improve your effectiveness is not always to work harder, but to rest harder and invoke God's help on your project. Just like the tithe puts a blessing on our money, honoring the Sabbath puts a blessing on our work and our time.

WEEK 46

WHAT ATTRACTS GOD?

"Has not my hand made all these things, and so they came into being?" declares the LORD. "This is the one I esteem: he who is humble and contrite in spirit, and trembles at my word."

Isaiah 66:2

If you were to stop a dozen people on the street and ask them: What is God looking for in humanity? You would probably get answers like: holiness, great faith, or even success. However, we see by this Scripture that is not necessarily true. Although all of these qualities would be wonderful to have, none of them are mentioned in the passage above. The above Scripture mentions three things that really attract God and draws Him to a person. It may come as a surprise to some and a real encouragement to others that God is not looking for superstars or people who have it all together, but simply people who are struggling with their sinful nature and searching for real answers.

The first thing the Scripture mentions is a person with a poor spirit. This is not talking about a poor person but rather a person who realizes that nothing he has can impress or influence God. It is really talking about a person who walks in humility—a person who realizes his or her spiritual poverty.

Another way to define this word "poor," is meek. Meekness is controlled strength. It is having the ability to bring judgment but choosing mercy. The qualities being talked about here are the qualities of those who realize they have needs beyond their ability to meet them. Again, this is not talking about poverty, which is a common result of our fallen nature, but a spiritual poverty where a person's heart is dry and needs refreshment. Praise God that this attitude attracts the living water of which, if we drink, we will never thirst again.

The second thing we see that attracts God is a person with a contrite spirit. The word "contrite" can be defined as sorrowful or dejected. Again this goes along with what was previously said. A contrite person is sorry for their sin and feels the scourge of guilt and condemnation, but does not have the ability to do anything about it. It was for this reason that God was touched with our sorrow and sent Jesus, His only Son, to be our Savior. Simply put, there is no other way out of our sorrow. Only Jesus can set us free and fills us with joy overflowing.

Pride pushes God away, but knowing we are weak always invites His strength.

Finally, this passage tells us that God is attracted to those who tremble at His Word. This means God is attracted to those who have a holy fear of Him and His Word. This does not mean we are to be afraid of God, but rather love God so much that we do not want to hurt or anger Him by falling into or continuing in sin.

All of the above qualities are not qualities admired or sought after by the world, but rather qualities of people who after walking with God and spending time in His presence, realize they still have much further to go. Pride pushes God away, but knowing we are weak always invites His strength. Perhaps you are feeling the weight of sin and struggle in your life. The enemy would like you to think the more honest you are, the more God will stay away. Nothing could be further from the truth! God is attracted to those who are transparent in their need and are willing to humble themselves and reach out to Him. Need by itself will not attract God, but need that reaches out in faith to God for forgiveness will always be met by a loving God who will forgive and cleanse us from our sin. Remember, it is not your strength that attracts God, but the reality that we are in desperate need of a Savior. This will bring Him quickly to your side.

WEEK 47

AND HE PRAYED AGAIN

He went away again the second time, and prayed, saying, O my Father, if this cup may not pass away from me, except I drink it, thy will be done.
Matthew 26:42 (KJV)

In this passage, we find Jesus in the Garden of Gethsemane with His disciples, praying for guidance regarding His upcoming crucifixion. Feeling the weight of what was ahead, Jesus pursued what was most natural—prayer. Knowing He was going to be put to death, He did not try to run or talk it over with His disciples, but rather tried to get alone with His Father and get a little prayer back-up from His friends. As for the prayer back-up from His disciples, it was more like sleeping with the enemy, but that is for a different writing. Over the years in Christian circles one of the big controversies has been, "Is it a lack of faith to pray more than once about a situation?" Let us take a look at this issue and see what the Bible actually teaches about it and how we can help shed some light on this thought.

The first thing we want to know about prayer is that more often than not prayer changes us. God's will for our lives has already been written in eternity. Whether or not we see or carry it out is another issue. In this situation, God's plan was for Jesus to die for the sins of the world. In reading this passage, Jesus would have preferred another plan, but His obedience won out over His desire. When it comes to praying more than once about a situation there are a few things we want to look at. First of all, the Bible teaches that **"...your Father knows what you need before you ask him" (Matthew 6:8).** So, if you want to get technical you do not have to pray even once. However, the Bible also teaches that **"You do not have because you do not ask" (James 4:2 NAS).** Therefore, that makes this argument null and void. In almost every situation, God requires that we humble ourselves and make our requests made known unto Him.

Through much prayer over a subject our hearts and minds are changed and become more like His.

As far as praying more than once, perhaps God does not need to hear it more than once. But we may have to say it more than once to believe that it has been taken care of. Paul prayed three times that the thorn in his flesh would be removed from him. God answered his prayer—the answer was "No," but there would be enough grace to deal with the problem (see II Corinthians 12:7-9). In Luke 18, the story about the persistent widow also makes it clear that God honors persistency in prayer. It was the widow's constant petitioning that moved the heart of the judge. Jesus, Himself, said that when we pray we should ask, seek, and then knock (see Matthew 7:7). This speaks to me of repetition and process.

As I said earlier, although God already knows our needs; many times we must learn how much we really are committed to seeing our prayers answered. Persistence in prayer is one way of seeing that. What may be gained most in our persistent prayer over the same situation is that God is able to give us His perspective on the situation. Through much prayer over a subject our hearts and minds are changed and become more like His. When we begin to see God's perspective about a situation, we then are able to understand why and how God is working things out in our lives. This brings peace and comfort to a situation.

In closing, it is important to note that when we humble ourselves before God in prayer by admitting our needs and our inabilities to meet those needs, we begin to open the door to God's storehouse. If you can believe your answer is on the way after the first time you pray, praise the Lord. However, it is pretty clear that God does not have a problem with us repeating ourselves as long as He does not have to repeat Himself.

WEEK 48

ALMOST

Then Agrippa said unto Paul, Almost thou persuadest me to be a Christian.
Acts 26:28 (KJV)

They say almost does not count for too much in this world, except maybe in horseshoes and darts. In fact, I cannot figure out why it even counts for much there. Is almost hitting the dartboard a good thing? The truth is it does not count for too much in God's kingdom either. You cannot almost be saved. You cannot almost obey God or almost stop committing adultery. In fact, "almost" often leads to a negative ending. For instance, "we almost saved his life" is not a good thing. The reason "almost" does not work in our Christian walk is because God requires commitment in whatever we do for Him. Whether it is beginning a new life in Christ or letting go of past sins, God expects us to give our whole heart in doing it.

We see in this passage that Paul had just finished giving a passionate plea for the souls of King Agrippa, Bernice, and Festus. He was standing before them on trial for his own life and yet, he was trying to save theirs. For some reason, Paul's pleading message for their souls to be saved did not totally change their hearts. Instead, he was met with the sad response of **"almost thou hast persuaded me to be a Christian."** Even Paul's reply to their "almost" was a last ditch effort to bring them to Jesus.

Nice try Paul—very persuasive—you *almost* had me. Almost can be a very dangerous word—a word that leaves a lot of room for the enemy to set up camp. Almost is a word that means we have left room for leaven to come in. It is giving 95 percent instead of 100 percent. Most importantly it is telling the enemy that there is still a possibility that we will serve him and not the Lord Jesus. When it comes to our walk with the Lord, almost is a word we do not want to have associated with our lives. So how do we take the "almosts" in our lives and turn them into sure things?

Jesus did not almost die on the cross, and you will not be able to almost serve God.

A clear look at God's Word will show us there is nothing that is almost about God. When He saw man floundering in sin, He paid the *full* price for us through the death of His only Son, Jesus. By the death of His Son, *all* things have been opened up to us in the heavenlies. Salvation is a gift for whosoever will come, not just a choice few. God has totally committed Himself to our success; now He is looking for a people who are totally committed and sold out to living for Him. God is a God who is all-knowing, all-powerful, and always present. There is nothing I can think of that is halfway or almost about God. He is simply everything we will always need Him to be.

Let us get back to "almost." Do you see why it cannot work in the kingdom? We are called to be followers of God and in doing so we will always be required to pay the full price. Nothing else will do. Paul knew it and that is why when King Agrippa said Paul had almost persuaded him to be a Christian, it was no compliment. Paul knew almost would not work because there was nothing almost about

Paul either. Even when he served Satan, he did it with all of his heart. When he met Jesus Christ on the road to Damascus, he knew what was required—total commitment. Jonah did not almost go to Nineveh. Jesus did not almost die on the cross, and you will not be able to almost serve God. It will take everything you have. The good news, however, is that God will give you everything it takes to do the job. All we must do is be willing to give it our all. God has promised to help us do the rest.

WEEK 49

FAVOR AS AN EXIT

"Now a young Hebrew was there with us,
a servant of the captain of the guard.
We told him our dreams, and he interpreted
them for us, giving each man the
interpretation of his dream.

And things turned out exactly as he
interpreted them to us: I was restored to my
position, and the other man was hanged."

So Pharaoh sent for Joseph, and he
was quickly brought from the dungeon.

Genesis 41:12-14

Most of the time when we discuss favor we talk about it as a door opener or an entrance. Favor might allow us into places we normally could not go. I would like to look at favor in a totally different way. You see, favor is not only an entrance, but can also be an exit. Favor will not only help us get into positions that the average person could not get into, but favor can also help get us out of situations to which we might not otherwise be able. The life of Joseph is a beautiful example of this.

After being falsely accused of rape by Potiphar's wife, Joseph was thrown into prison. God used this time in prison to further increase both the character and the favor in Joseph's life (see Genesis 39:19-23). It is important to see that God can bring favor to us in all seasons of our lives—both the good ones and bad. Favor does not always mean smooth sailing, but rather a strong vessel. The times we need favor the most are not the good times when we can navigate the waters of life, but those times when we are in fear for our lives and all eyes are on us. Paul had favor on his way to Rome on a ship that was destined for disaster. It was there the Word of the Lord came to him, bringing wisdom and comfort to those sailing with him (see Acts 27:21-26).

> *God can bring favor to us in all seasons of our lives—both the good ones and bad.*

Favor with God will often bring favor with man. While Joseph was in prison, he walked in great favor. His favor was so great in prison that he was trusted with the lives of two of Pharaoh's officers—the butler and the baker. While in his care one night, they had dreams that they could not understand. The next morning, when Joseph saw them and saw the sad look on their faces, he asked them what the problem was. Their response was they had dreams that they could not interpret. Knowing that he had a gift from God to interpret dreams, he asked them to tell him their dreams. Shortly after hearing their dreams, he was able to give each of them the interpretation. At that time, Joseph made a simple request to the chief butler: When you are restored to the kingdom, please remember me in prison and put in a good word to the king for him to release me.

There are a few insights about favor that we want to notice here. First, Joseph walked in great favor at a very difficult time in his life. The flow of God's favor does not stop when times get tough. Know that wherever you are today God is able to grant you favor with those around you. Second, we see that Joseph's gift enabled him to minister to those who eventually helped obtain his release. Proverbs 18:16 states **"a man's gift makes room for him"** (NKJV). We see this very clearly here in the life of Joseph. Had he not had this gift to interpret dreams, he very likely may have remained in prison.

Finally, we see that it was Joseph's favor with those two men that eventually brought him his freedom from prison. So we see, when necessary, favor can be an exit from a very hard place. Perhaps you are sitting today in a hard place—even a prison of your own making. Remember, it is never too late to begin to obey God, asking Him to bless you with His favor. It could be the key that unlocks the prison doors of your life and puts you back on the road to reach your destiny.

WEEK 50

THE MYTH OF FREEDOM

"Then you will know the truth, and the truth will set you free."

They answered him, "We are Abraham's descendants and have never been slaves of anyone. How can you say that we shall be set free?"

Jesus replied, "I tell you the truth, everyone who sins is a slave to sin.

Now a slave has no permanent place in the family, but a son belongs to it forever.

So if the Son sets you free, you will be free indeed.

John 8:32-36

As Americans, we have been taught all of our lives about the value of freedom. We have learned to live in freedom and we are quick to die for our freedom. I am reminded of the words of Patrick Henry who said, "Give me liberty or give me death." I wonder if he ever thought about the fact that if not handled properly, our liberty or freedom as we will call it in this writing, could kill us? Like everything else in this world, freedom comes with a price. As a nation we are now starting to deal with the fallout of chasing after freedoms rather than God. The freedoms we have fought and died for can become the very things that put us into bondage.

Some two hundred years after becoming a nation founded on freedom of worship, we have developed into a country that worships freedom. We are all free to do our own thing. I am reminded of Proverbs 14:12 which says: **"There is a way that seems right to man, but in the end it leads to death."** Even our Constitution guarantees us the ability to pursue happiness and not necessarily God. Here we see part of the problem. I could think of many things that could bring me happiness temporarily, but could very well keep me out of heaven eternally. Yes, there are many things that can bring me happiness but put me in bondage.

There are many things that can bring me happiness but put me in bondage.

It should not come as a surprise that America has become a country that if necessary, puts each individual's desires and freedoms before God. Do we want a country that guarantees everyone freedom while these freedoms slowly put everyone into bondage? Or, do we want to be a country that restrains itself when necessary, yet remains made up of free people? Is freedom just the ability to say yes to everything, or are we also free to say no? Unity must be based on all people having some common values. Yet, the only common thread we seem to be left with is that we all want to be free—to do our own thing. Unity not based on common value leads to confusion and eventual destruction.

Jesus stated very clearly that there was a connection between knowing truth and having freedom. Before we go any further with this thought, we must clarify that the truth

Jesus was talking about was the written Word of God, the Bible. In order for men to be free, their lives have to be lined up with biblical principles and have a relationship with the God of these principles. In the Scripture stated above we see the process. To be a follower of God, a disciple, you must continue in the Word. In other words, you have to have an ongoing love affair with the Word of God and the God of the Word. This was the first step given in the journey toward freedom.

Jesus then goes on to say after continuing in the Word, you shall know the truth and the truth shall make you free (see John 8:32). Here we clearly see the connection that Jesus gives between freedom and truth. True freedom is based on the knowledge of God's Word. That is the price we must pay for freedom. I thank God for a free country, but more importantly, I thank God that I am free. In many ways, America today has become a haven for every bondage known to man—all in the name of freedom. Freedom not based on the truth of God's Word can be very dangerous.

WEEK 51

LOVE AND RESPECT

who despises a vile man but honors those who fear the LORD, who keeps his oath even when it hurts

Psalm 15:4

I recently overheard a conversation between two women that caught my attention. The one lady was telling the other that she truly loved her father but was feeling very guilty because she could not respect him. She went on to say that her father had cheated on her mother, had stolen things from places he had worked, and in general, was a very unsavory character, which brings us to the point of this writing. In life there will be some people we love but cannot respect because their behavior or their lifestyle will not allow it. What we want to see in this writing is that there is a difference between honoring and respecting a person's position and their personality or behavior.

To begin with, the young lady was a Christian who was struggling with unnecessary guilt. She had good reason to love her father, but no good reason to respect him because his behavior was quite sinful. One of the definitions of the word "respect" is "to hold in special esteem." It is important that we see that although God loves the sinner, He does not love the sin, nor does He hold it in high regard. Since we are supposed to be followers of Christ, it would make perfect sense that this woman would love her father, but not appreciate or hold in high esteem his behavior. God's command toward our fellow man (and that includes family members) is that we love them, but not necessarily respect or hold in high esteem all the things that they do.

When the Bible talks about honoring and respecting our parents and those in authority over us, it has to do with their position in our lives, not necessarily their behavior or lifestyle. We honor our parents because they have a God-given place of authority in our lives. We honor and respect the office of the President of the United States, even if the President's behavior has been ungodly. We can love all of the above because of the love of Christ in us. We also understand that God works through imperfect, delegated authority. A person does not have to be perfect for us to be obedient or respectful towards them. Once again, the big difference is that respect has to do with position, not always people and their behavior.

Respect has to do with position, not always people and their behavior.

A beautiful example of this is the relationship between David and King Saul. Although King Saul had seemingly gone mad and was chasing David throughout the land trying to kill him, David would never raise a hand against him. At one point when he could have killed him because he and his armorbearer had fallen asleep, David, instead, cut off a small piece of his clothing. For that action, David's conscience pierced him because he had disrespected the office of king.

He was not respecting or honoring Saul, but the God-given authority that Saul had in his position as king.

In closing, there will be times when we, like David, will be tested as to whether we have respect for a person in spite of their behavior or lifestyle. Two things are important to remember here. First, God has called us to be a people of love. It is a commandment to love one another (see John 13:34). The reason God can make that demand of us is because He will give us the love to love the unlovely. As far as honor or respect, they are earned by the good behavior and the virtues of an individual. If you cannot honor a person for those reasons, try to be mindful of the position they hold in your life. Often, we will be asked by God to show respect to a position, not a personality. When you cannot respect a person, know that through the love of Christ you can show love, which may open a door for you to share the changing power of Christ with them.

WEEK 52

THE TROUBLE WITH FAVOR

And when his brethren saw that their father loved him more than all his brethren, they hated him, and could not speak peaceably unto him.
Genesis 37:4 (KJV)

The way people look at those whom God has favored is sometimes a funny thing. It is not always pretty nor is it always Christian. People love to help and bless a person who is struggling, and that is as it should be. It is surprising, however, to see how people will treat you when you start to get blessed. Favor with God will often bring favor with man. Sometimes, however, favor with God will bring trouble with man—especially the brethren. Other Christians will sometimes get very envious over you getting blessed—almost as if God took their blessing and gave it to you. If favor had a color I would have to guess it would be green—green with envy. Let us look at the life of Joseph to see how walking in favor does not necessarily mean walking without problems.

As the son of his old age, Jacob was quite proud of his young son, Joseph. To make sure everyone knew it, he gave him a coat of many colors. Besides looking like the favored son of his father, God had given Joseph a dream in which he showed Joseph that one day all of his brothers would be bowing down to him. Because his favor was so great with both their earthly father as well as their heavenly Father, it incited anger in those around him. So believing that he was the favorite child (this may or may not have been the case) of their father and a little bit of a braggart, they plotted for his demise.

The next place we find Joseph is in a pit, where he was left by his brothers to die. Soon after that, his brothers began to feel guilty about the diabolical plan to kill their own flesh and blood and decided to sell him into slavery—not a great place to be, but better than dead. Without a gripe or complaint, Joseph accepted his fate and began to excel at his job in the house of his new boss, Potiphar, Captain of the guard for the Pharaoh (see Genesis 37:3-36; 39:1-6).

Having favor with God does not always translate into having favor with all men.

Let us stop here for a moment and notice one thing. Joseph's brothers began to hate him when they saw the favor of God and the abundant love of their father in his life. I want to add another thing—I do not believe that Jacob loved Joseph any more than the others, only that he showed it more, which could be a good lesson to us all.

Very often the same people that love you when you are pathetic will be envious of you when you are blessed. Nothing will get people's attention, especially religious people, more than a man walking in favor and the blessings of God. Unfortunately, it is not godly attention we are always talking about. So do not be surprised if everyone does not celebrate your blessings. Daniel walked in such great favor in Babylon that he was raised above his peers, despite the fact that he was a foreigner. Again, I want to point out that although Daniel lived an exemplary life and they could find no fault with him under normal circumstances, this did not stop those around him from plotting against him. Although their plot was eventually uncovered, we see again that having favor with God does not always translate into having favor with men (see Daniel 6).

If the favor with God is causing you trouble with those around you, here are a few quick insights to live by. First, always use your favor to bless others. It is hard to dislike someone who is trying to bless you. Never brag about what God is doing for you or through you. The Bible tells us to **"Rejoice with them that do rejoice, and weep with them that weep" (Romans 12:15 KJV).** Someone holding on by a thread may not be able to handle your blessings at that moment. Only share as God leads you and share with others who are equally as blessed.

Finally, understand the favor of God can sometimes be a lonely walk and can cause misunderstanding with those around you. Walk in mercy and grace knowing that sometimes favor can be a heavy burden to carry.

Request a *FREE* MorningStar Resource Catalog!